BEMBÉ DELLINGER ARCHITECTS

Bilder und Pläne | pictures and plans

1999 - 2009

SpringerWienNewYork

>49 >674 **000**

DOPPELHAUS AN DER SONNENLEITE

Semi-detached house on Sonnenleite

1999
Schondorf
1685 cbm
fertiggestellt | completed
privat | private
LPH 1-8 G/F/A

>56 >675 **001**

WOHNEN AM REIHERWEG

Living on Reiherweg

2002
Schondorf
2013 cbm
fertiggestellt | completed
privat | private
LPH 1-8 G/F/A

>72 >676 **002**

HAUS HL

House HL

2003
Schondorf
920 cbm
fertiggestellt | completed
privat | private
LPH 1-8 G/F/A

401

RUDOLF STEINER - SCHULE

Rudolf Steiner school

2000
München - Daglfing
28.000 cbm
Wettbewerb 2.Preis | competition 2.price
Rudolf-Steiner-Schulverein München e.V.
LPH 1-2 G/F

>78 >677 **003**

ATELIER IM CURRYPARK

Studio in Currypark

2003
Riederau
665 cbm
fertiggestellt | completed
privat | private
LPH 1-8 G/F/A

402

GRUNDSCHULE MÜNCHEN - SENDLING

Munich - Sendling primary school

2000
München - Sendling
30.500 cbm
Wettbewerb 4.Preis | competition 4.price
Landeshauptstadt München
LPH 1-2 G/F

Die Bank lieh uns Geld für Grundstück und Gebäude. So konnten wir unser erstes Haus bauen. Zwei Wohneinheiten, jeder Zeit real teilbar. Ein langes und schmales Haus mit vielen Zimmern folgt dem abschüssigen Hang. Alle Räume nach Süden gerichtet auf die große Wiese, wie es sich gehört. Die Terrassen weit voneinander entfernt, das Nebeneinander im Garten entspannt. Das Haus ist seit 10 Jahren vermietet und 7 Kinder sind darin groß geworden.
The bank lent us the money for the plot and the house. We were therefore able to develop our first building. Two units, separable at any time. A long narrow building on the incline of the hill, with a sequence of rooms, all facing south, looking out onto a big field – exactly the way it should be. The terraces are set far apart; the situation in the garden is relaxed. The house has now been let for 10 years and 7 children have grown up in it.

Unser erstes Bauwerk erschien der Bauverwaltung im nach hinein zu lang geraten und so unterstützte sie den Wunsch unserer Bauherren, statt einem planerisch vorgesehenen Doppelhaus zwei einzelne Gebäude zu errichten. Es entstand eine kleine Gruppe von kompakten Volumen um einen gemeinsamen Platz. Die Wohnbereiche liegen großzügig geöffnet zu den privaten Gärten, die Nebenräume verschlossener am Platz. Überhohe drehbare Holzlamellen filtern die wechselnde Kontaktfreudigkeit der Bewohner.
The local government thought that the building we had previously planned was too long and, therefore, supported our clients' wish to plan two single-family homes instead of the proposed semi-detached house. The result is a small group of compact buildings arranged around a communal square. The fully glazed living areas look out onto the private gardens; the functional rooms, slightly more enclosed, towards the square. High timber fences, with rotating lamella, adjust to suit the mood of the residents.

Die liebgewonnene Wohnung in einem Gebäude des Architekten Vorhölzer wollte man eigentlich nicht verlassen. Sie war jedoch zu klein geworden. Interesse für ein Haus aus den 60ern, das man aber nicht kaufen konnte. So entschloss sich das Lehrerehepaar zum Neubau am Ortsrand mit schönem Blick über die weite Flur. Ein schlichtes Siedlungshaus, archetypisch, wie es der Bebauungsplan vorsah. Das Souterrain mit eigenem Zugang für die erwachsen werdenden Kinder, das Dachgeschoss für die Eltern und die Ebene dazwischen für das gemeinsame Leben.
It was difficult for them to let go of the apartment they had come to love. However, the space in the building designed by the architect Vorhölzer no longer met their needs. A 60's building was interesting, but not affordable. For this reason, the teacher couple decided to plan their own house on the outskirts of town with a view across the fields. A simple dwelling, with archetypal features like those in housing estates, as foreseen in the development plan. A basement level with its own access for the growing-up children, the top floor for the parents and a level in between for communal living.

Ein spezielles Haus. Ein Haus für die eigene Verwandtschaft, mit der Möglichkeit, auch den künftigen Generationen noch Spielraum zu lassen. Zunächst als Atelier und Wochenendhaus genutzt, musste es pflegeleicht und robust sein. Gleichzeitig variabel genug für Kommendes. Ein Haus an dem viel heimisch ist und Einiges riskiert wurde, was man vielleicht so nur am eigenen Objekt verwirklichen kann.
A special house – a house for one's own relatives with sufficient leeway for future generations. At first only used as a studio and weekend house, it had to be hard wearing and low maintenance. However, at the same time, flexible enough to adapt to later needs. A house with lots of personality and a house with lots of risks taken on design – something you can only do in your own home.

>106 >678

004
AUFSTOCKUNG EINES HAUSES
Additional storey for a house

2004
Utting
769 cbm
fertiggestellt | completed
privat | private
LPH 1-8 G/F/A

>114 >679

005
ATELIER BAUER
Studio Bauer

2003
Grafing
769 cbm
fertiggestellt | completed
privat | private
LPH 1-4 G

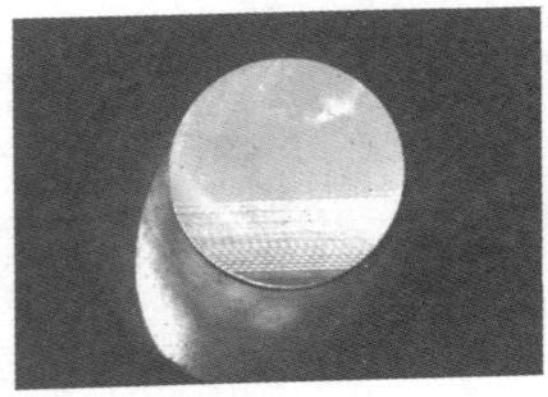

>122 >680

403
DIÖEZESANKURIE ROTTENBURG
Rottenburg Bishop's Diocese

2002
Rottenburg
25.200 cbm
Wettbewerb Ankauf | competition purchase
Bistum Rottenburg
LPH 1-2 G/F

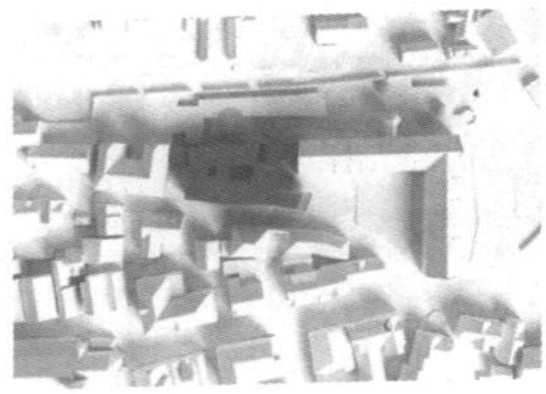

006
HAUS KT
House KT

2002
Steinebach
1.064 cbm
fertiggestellt | completed
privat | private
LPH 5-8 G/F/A

>130 >681

007
HAUS MIT PRAXIS
Single-family home with surgery

2001
Diessen
1.110 cbm
fertiggestellt | completed
privat | private
LPH 1-8 G/F/A

404
KINDERHAUS RIEDERAU
Riederau childcare centre

2002
Riederau
3.500 cbm
Wettbewerb | competition
Markt Diessen am Ammersee
LPH 1-2 G/F

In den Nachkriegsjahren entstanden am Ammersee viele Wochenendhäuser. So auch dieses Haus für den Vater unserer Bauherren, einen Arzt und passionierten Jäger, der hier seine Jagd hatte. Für die kommende Generation sollte die Ferienwohnung erhalten bleiben und für die Generation im Ruhestand um eine Wohneinheit ergänzt werden. Das Gebäude wurde in der Länge für den jetzigen Aufgang ein wenig erweitert und ein neues Geschoss in leichter Holzkonstruktion über den Bestand gestülpt. Ein offener und heller Lebensraum mit traumhaftem Blick über den See.
Lots of weekend houses were developed at Lake Ammersee in the post-war period. The same applies to this house, which was developed for our clients' father, a doctor and passionate hunter, with his hunting grounds right here. The holiday apartment was to be maintained for the next generation and a new dwelling unit was to be added for the now retired generation. The length of the building was increased to integrate the access to the new storey, a light timber construction, which has been slipped over the existing building. The result is a very open and light space with a breathtaking view across the lake.

Ein Haus für einen befreundeten Holzbildhauer, Ersatz für den bisherigen Zirkuswagen. Um Fenster herumgebaut, die es schon gab. Das Bauen entwickelte sich langsam und informell. Im Souterrain eine große Werkstatt zum Schreinern, auf dem Carport ein 5 m hohes Atelier zum Holzbildhauen und im Garten ein großes Becken zum Schwimmen. Nur das eigentlich geforderte Satteldach wurde noch nicht gebaut.
A house for a friend, a wood carver; a substitute for a home in a circus wagon. Built around windows that had already been obtained. The building work was slow and informal. A large workshop for joinery work in the basement, a 5 m-high studio for wood carving on top of the carport and a large swimming pool in the garden. Everything except the requested saddle roof has been built.

Die Diözesankurie des Bischöflichen Ordinariats sollte im historischen Gebäudeensemble am Rande der Altstadt Rottenburgs zusammengeführt und das Archiv erweitert werden. Wir versuchten mit dem Neubau historisch bebaute Flächen wieder aufzufüllen. Tiefe Einschnitte, vergleichbar Altstadtgassen, bringen Licht und Luft in den Neubau. Der historische Burggraben blieb bewusst unbebaut, die historische Altstadt sollte wieder lesbar werden.
The aim was to integrate the Bishop's residence into the historical building cluster on the edge of Rottenburg's old town and to enlarge the archive. We tried to refill originally developed space with new structures. Deep crevices, like the little alleys in the old town, enable light and air to flood into the new building. The historical moat has deliberately been left open in order to highlight the boundary of the old town.

Ein Haus für ein Ehepaar, beide Heilpraktiker, zum Wohnen mit den 4 Kindern und zum Arbeiten. Alles unter einem Dach, so wie es früher einmal war. Das schmale Grundstück am Ortsrand ließ nur ein Staffeln der Bereiche zu. Carport, Eingangshof und Praxis im Norden und Wohnen nach Süden mit freiem Blick auf Wiesen und Weiher. Die Überschuppung der beiden Dächer lässt das Sonnenlicht auch in die nördlichen Praxisräume fallen. Die ökologischen Ansprüche der Bauherren führen zu einem massiven Holzbau mit Gründach, Innenräumen mit Lehmputz und Solaranlage mit Restwärmeerzeugung aus Holzpellets.
A house for a married couple, both alternative medicine practitioners, to live in with their 4 children and to work in. Everything under one roof, as it used to be in former times. Due to the narrow plot on the outskirts of town, the areas had to be staggered. Carport, entrance area and surgery in the north and, to the south, living accommodation with an unspoilt view of the fields and pond. The staggered roofs enable light to reach into the surgery positioned furthest north. Our clients' ecological demands are expressed in the timber construction with roof planting, the lime plaster on the interior walls and a solar plant to provide warmth; a wood pellet burner functions as an additional heat source.

>142 >682

405
NRW - BANK MÜNSTER
Münster NRW - Bank

2005
Münster
30.500 cbm
Wettbewerb Ankauf | competition purchase
NRW - Bank Münster
LPH 1-2 G/F

>146 >683

008
HAUS W
House W

2003
Pullach
1.555 cbm
fertiggestellt | completed
privat | private
LPH 1-8 G/F/A

009
WOHNBEBAUUNG KIRCHSTEIG
Kirchsteig residential area

1999
Diessen
1.440 cbm
fertiggestellt | completed
privat | private
LPH 1-8 G

010
SCHULERWEITERUNG ORTENBURG
Ortenburg school extension

2000
Ortenburg
3.647 cbm
fertigggetellt | completed
Prof. Starzner für Evang. Erziehungsstiftung Ortenburg
LPH 5 G

>158 >684

406
ERWEITERUNG DER STADTHALLE
Town hall extension

2005
Penzberg
16.202 cbm
Wettbewerb 4.Preis | competition 4.price
Stadt Penzberg
LPH 1-2 G/F

011
ANBAU EINES WOHNRAUMES
Living room extension

2000
München
120 cbm
Studie | study
privat | private
LPH 1-3 G

Der historische Altbau der NRW-Bank in Münster musste erweitert werden. Ein kristallin anmutender Baukörper umgreift den Altbau. Der auskragende Kopf formuliert den neuen Eingang. Ein steinerner Sockel nimmt beinahe das ganze Grundstück ein.
The historical building housing the NRW Bank in Münster had to be enlarged. A glass building with a crystalline appearance wraps itself around the old structure. The protruding element functions as a new entrance. The solid base takes up most of the plot.

Die Gemeinde Pullach ist stolz auf ihre Baubeschränkungen. Strenge Auflagen zu Dachform und Höhenentwicklung führten zu einem Haus mit zwei Bereichen. Umgeben von zweigeschossigen, hohen und lichten Aufenthaltsräumen liegt ein innerer dreigeschossiger Kern mit reduzierten Raumhöhen für Nebenräume und der Dachkanzel als Ort für Rückzug und Arbeit.
The municipality of Pullach is proud of its building restrictions. Strict regulations regarding roof shape and heights led to a house with two areas. A two-storey element with high, light living and sleeping quarters surrounds a three-storey core with lower ceiling heights for functional rooms and a roof studio as a place to retreat and work.

Unser Ziel war es die Stadthalle der 20er Jahre wieder auf ihre elegante und zurückhaltende Erscheinung der Erbauungszeit zurückzuführen. Der Erweiterungsbau legt sich mit einem Schwung um den Altbau und schiebt sich weit in den neuen Platz. Das Ensemble ist in Weiß und historischem Hellblau gefasst.
Our aim was to return the town hall, which was built in the 20's, to its elegant but slightly reserved appearance as found in the original building. The extension envelops the old building in a single grand gesture and reaches out far into the new square. The architectural ensemble is kept in white and traditional light blue.

012
HAUS CF
House CF

1999
Langwied
1.060 cbm
fertiggestellt | completed
privat | private
LPH 1-8 G/F/A

>162 >685

013
WOHNBEBAUUNG LACHEN - BIRKENALLEE
Lachen-Birkenallee residential area

2007
Diessen
4.888 cbm
fertiggestellt | completed
Bauherrengemeinschaft Kithier
LPH 1-8 G/F/A

>180 >686

014
HOLZSTOSS
Stack of logs

2001
Landsberg
11 cbm
fertiggestellt | completed
Wessobrunner Kreis
LPH 1-8 G

>184 >687

015
WOHNANLAGE GARTENSTRASSE
Gartenstrasse residential complex

2007
Greifenberg
4.375 cbm
fertiggestellt | completed
privat | private
LPH 1-8 G/A

016
UMBAU BAUMANN
Baumann refurbishment

1999
Moorenweis
515 cbm
fertiggestellt | completed
privat | private
LPH 1-8 G/F/A

017
WOHNRAUMERWEITERUNG
Extension

2003
Solln
168 cbm
fertiggestellt | completed
privat | private
LPH 1-4 G

Eine Siedlung ohne Bauträger und Spekulation sollte entstehen. Eine Siedlung, die der Grundstückseigentümer auch nach Jahren noch gerne betritt. Das Grundstück war da, zwei Wohneinheiten sollten für die Töchter erhalten bleiben, für den Rest suchte man Mitbauherren. Das Konzept war entwickelt, das Erscheinungsbild sollte einheitlich bleiben, innen waren alle individuellen Wünsche erlaubt. Verblüffend homogen und friedfertig entstand in gemeinschaftlicher Anstrengung die Siedlung.

The plan was to develop a residential area without involvement of a property developer and without speculative operations. A residential area which the owner of the plot would enjoy walking through years later. The plot was there, two dwelling units were to be retained for the daughters, and clients for the remaining plots were selected. A concept had been established, the outer appearance was supposed to be uniform, the design of the interior was up to each client. A surprisingly homogeneous, peaceful area has been created through teamwork with the other homeowners.

Die Ausstellung „Neues Bauen in den Alpen" musste angekündigt werden. Es durfte nicht viel kosten und sollte aufmerken lassen. Ein Holzstoß aus geliehenen Balken, lang und breit wie ein Pkw in einer Parkbucht, mit Schrift aus 30kg Nägel, von uns selbst eingeschlagen.

The exhibition „New Buildings in the Alps" had to be advertised. It had to be inexpensive, but eye-catching. A pile of borrowed logs, as long and wide as a car. Located in a parking bay with lettering consisting of 30 kg of nails, which we hammered in ourselves.

In unmittelbarer Nähe unseres Büros eine kleine Siedlung aus fünf Häusern für einen Gartenbauunternehmer und seine Söhne. Vorgaben zur Wirtschaftlichkeit und zur Ökologie waren bestimmend. Auf alles Überflüssige wurde verzichtet und auf das Notwendige sich konzentriert. Eine Türe in der Wand zum Betreten des Hauses, ein großzügiger Raum zum Leben mit einem großen Fenster in den Garten, knappe Zimmern für die Kinder und ein kleiner Bereich für die Eltern. Ein Lichthof im Keller für Gäste oder zum Arbeiten. Eine Farbe je Haus. Die Autos stehen außerhalb. Alle Grundrisse sind gleich, situativ je nach Ausrichtung nur gedreht oder gespiegelt. Eine eigene Welt inmitten des kleinen oberbayerischen Dorfes.

In immediate vicinity of our office there is a small residential area consisting of five houses for a landscape contractor and his sons. Requirements regarding the feasibility and ecology were decisive. Anything deemed superfluous was abandoned; the necessities determined the design. A door in the wall to access the house, a spacious room to live in with large windows overlooking the garden, small rooms for the children and a small area for the parents. A light well to illuminate the basement area for guests and work. A different colour for each house. The cars are parked beyond the plot. All floor plans are the same, but rotated or mirrored, depending on the orientation. A different world in the middle of a little Upper Bavarian village.

>196 >688

018
HAUS E
House E

2006
Tutzing
1.704 cbm
fertiggestellt | completed
privat | private
LPH 1-8 G/F/A

019
ANBAU EINES SWIMMING POOLS
Swimming pool extension

2004
Diessen
620 cbm
Studie | study
privat | private
LPH 1-2 G

>210 >689

020
HAUS K
House K

2000
Fischen
1.365 cbm
fertiggestellt | completed
privat | private
LPH 1-8 G/F/A

>220 >690

407
WOHNBEBAUUNG SEDANSTRASSE
Sedanstrasse residential area

2005
Straubing
25.500 cbm
Wettbewerb | competition
Städtische Wohnungsbau GmbH
LPH. 1-2 G/F

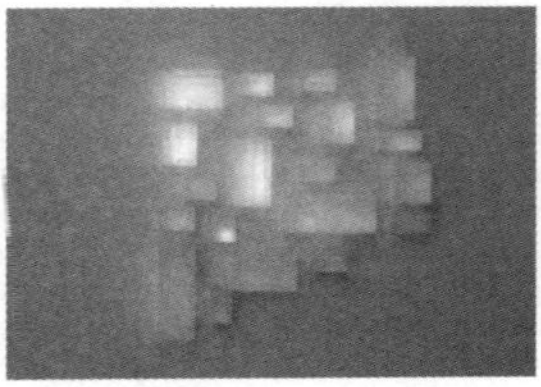

021
HAUS BL
House BL

2004
Schondorf
1.554 cbm
fertiggestellt | completed
privat | private
LPH 1-8 G

022
DACHAUFBAU
Roof extension

2006
München Bogenhausen
563 cbm
Studie | study
privat | private
LPH 1-2 G

Der Fernblick hatte es den Bauherren angetan. Hier, und genau hier musste das Wohnzimmer liegen. So knickte sich das Haus um diese Vorgabe. Spiralförmig, dem Ausblick folgend, vom Freisitz im Garten hinauf zum erwünschten Bergblick. Höhlenförmige Dusch- und WC- Bereiche im Kern stehen im Gegensatz zu hohen und weiten Wohnbereichen. Eine zentrale Spindeltreppe verbindet alle Geschosse und bildet eine alternative Erschließung zum großzügigen Umgang.
The clients were absolutely taken by the view. The living room was to be placed here and only here. Hence, the zigzag shape to meet this demand. Spiral-shaped to take advantage of the view, from the outside seating area in the garden to the desired mountain view. Cave-like shower and toilet facilities in the core are the exact opposite to the high and spacious living areas. A central spiral staircase connects all levels and is a contrast to the alternative access via the generously laid-out surrounding path.

Die Vorbilder lagen in Vorarlberg und in der Schweiz, oder auch nur im Stadel und den Einfirsthöfen nebenan. Ein Haus, reduziert in Materialität und Form, am Rande der Ortschaft. Außen bekleidet mit unbehandelter Lärche, innen Wände und Decken aus rohem Beton. Ein Grundriss, so variabel, dass er das Wohnen mit den damals schon fast erwachsenen Kindern möglich machte und mit einer Teilung der Wohnung auf deren Auszug reagieren konnte.
This one was modelled on the architecture in Vorarlberg, Austria, and Switzerland or quite simply that of the Stadel (barn) and the other single ridge structures next door. A totally reduced, simple shaped building on the outskirts of the village. Sheathed with untreated larch on the exterior; walls and ceilings in exposed concrete in the interior. A totally flexible layout which enabled living with the, almost grown-up, children, but capable of being divided into separate units when they leave home.

Wohnkuben in extremer Dichte. Fortschreibung von Altstadt und Position gegen die Zeile. Wiederholung von Form und Material, Unterscheidung in Fläche und Höhe. Derart zusammengesetzt, dass jedes Haus zu seinem Recht kommt: Licht, Luft, Privatheit und Öffentlichkeit.
Extremely dense cube houses. As an extension of the old town and our response to the terraces. Repetitive in format and materials, however, differing in size and height. Arranged in a way that every building gets exactly what it needs: Light, air, privacy and space.

408
WOHNEN UND REITEN
Living and riding

2006
Breitenbrunn
50.143 cbm
Wettbewerb 1.Preis | competition 1.price
privater Bauherr
LPH. 1- 2 G/F

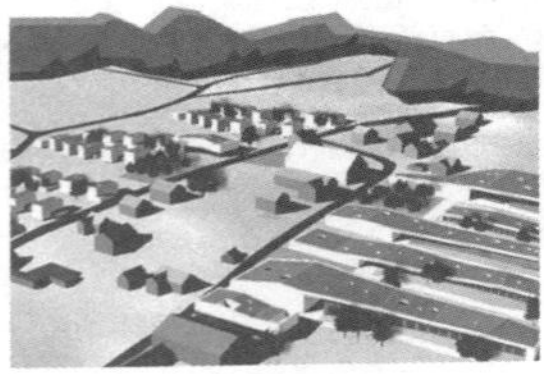

023
HAUS W2
House W2

2004
Icking
993 cbm
Studie | study
privat | private
LPH 1-2 G

>224 >691

024
WOHNBEBAUUNG PÖCKING
Pöcking residential complex

2009
Pöcking
6.602 cbm
im bau | in constrution
privat | private
LPH 1-8 G/F/A

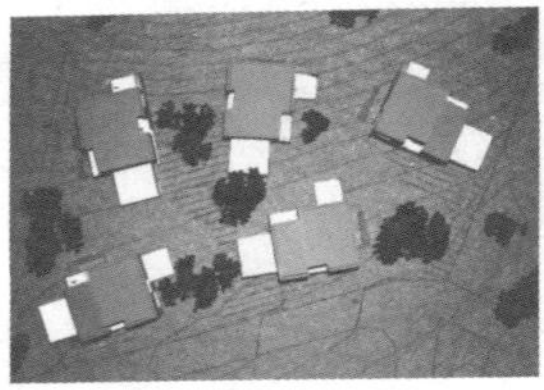

025
HALLE LÜCKE
Lücke hall

2003
Greifenberg
2.120 cbm
studie | study
privat | private
LPH 1-3 G

>234 >692

026
HAUS Z
House Z

2006
Eresing
1.196 cbm
fertiggestellt | completed
privat | private
LPH 1-8 G/F/A

>242 >693

409
EUROPÄISCHE SCHULE
European school

2006
München Neuperlach
68.592 cbm
Wettbewerb 3.Preis | competition 3.price
Staatliches Bauamt München
LPH 1-2 G/F

Ein Südhang mit Bachaue in einem beliebten Wohngebiet in der Nähe des Starnberger Sees. Der Grundstücksbesitzer als Nachbar. Ein Konzept mit fünf Baukörpern, spielerisch verteilt dem Hang folgend. Zwei Grundstücke frei verkauft, drei vom Bauherrn selber bebaut. Die Baukörper, als Typus entwickelt, mit sich wiederholenden Elementen und nach Notwendigkeit gedreht oder gespiegelt.
A south-facing slope with a stream in a popular residential area close to Lake Starnberg. The owner of the plot right next door. A concept with five elements scattered across the slope in a playful way. Two of the plots have been sold undeveloped; three of them have been developed by the client. The volume has been designed as a prototype with repetitive elements, which are simply rotated or mirrored according to demand.

Ein Haus im Neubaugebiet und nach Bauvorschrift mit Kniestock und Satteldach. Der Typus traditioneller Holzlegen mit asymmetrischem Dach („Maulaufreissern"), auf einer Seite geschlossen, auf der anderen Seite weit geöffnet, erschien uns gut geeignet. Verschlossen im Norden liegen die Nebenräume und großzügig offen zum Garten die Wohnräume. Das Innere loftartig mit hohen, offenen Raumeindrücken. Die dunkle Farbe der Holzverschalung wirkt elegant und so ganz anders in der bunten Umgebung.
A house in a new housing estate built according to building regulations with a jamb wall and saddle roof. We favoured the asymmetric roof traditionally applied to log stores, closed on one side and opened up generously on the other. The functional rooms closed in the north; the living rooms open to the garden. The inside is like a loft with high ceilings and an open character. The dark colour of the timber sheathing looks elegant and is a total contrast to its colourful surroundings.

Die bestehende Schule ist in Sichtmauerwerk gebaut. Auch der vorgeschlagene Erweiterungsbau interpretiert den Ziegel. Eine homogene Materialschicht bekleidet einheitlich Decken, Wände und Böden. Perforationen im Verband des Mauerwerks entmaterialisieren die tektonische Schicht und laden die zugeordneten Räume mit eigener Lichtstimmung und Atmosphäre auf.
The current school is built in fair-faced brickwork. The proposed extension also interprets the brick. A homogeneous skin of masonry evenly covers ceilings, walls and floors. Perforations in the bond dematerialise the tectonic layer and create different moods and atmospheres in the rooms beyond.

027
HAUS G
House G

2004
Herrsching
997 cbm
Studie | study
privat | private
LPH 1-4 G

028
HAUS WL
House WL

2005
Rieden
1.426 cbm
Studie | study
privat | private
LPH 1-2 G

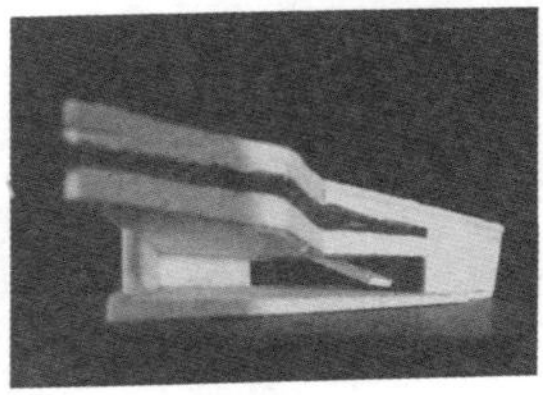

>248 >694 **029**
ZWILLINGSHAUS GRAFRATH
Grafrath twin house

2007
Grafrath
2.394 cbm
fertiggestellt | completed
privat | private
LPH 1-8 G/F/A

>264 >695 **410**
JUGENDHAUS DER VERSTÄNDIGUNG
Youth centre for communication

2006
Oberschleissheim
11.550 cbm
Wettbewerb | competition
privater Bauherr
LPH 1-2 G/F

>272 >696 **030**
ALTER SPORTPLATZ SCHONDORF
Schondorf former sports ground

2004
Schondorf
23.544 cbm
Studie | study
Gemeinde Schondorf | community Schondorf
LPH 1-2 G/F/A

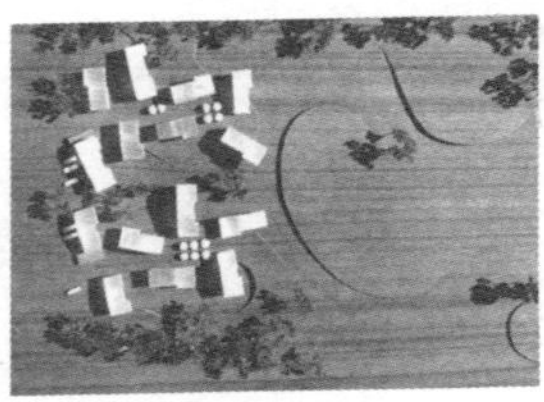

411
STUDENTENWOHNHEIM FREIMANN
Freimann student dormitory

2007
München - Freimann
13.146 cbm
Wettbewerb 2.Preis | competition 2.price
Josef Memminger
LPH 1-2 G/F

Ein steiler Hang, eingezwickt zwischen Fluss im Nord-Westen und hohem Buchenwald im Süd-Osten. Schon einige Planer haben sich an diesem Grundstück versucht. Es war günstig zu erwerben trotz traumhaftem Blick auf Fluss und Auenwald. Jetzt parkt man im Untergeschoss auf Höhe der Straße und steigt über Arbeits- und Schlafgeschoss hinauf ins Licht zum Wohnen in den Baumwipfeln. Im Fluss stehen die Fische, auf der Terrasse die Rehe.

A steep slope, wedged between a river in the northwest and a beech wood in the southeast. Several planners have made an attempt on this plot. It was cheap despite the incredible view of the river and floodplain woodland. Now you park in the basement on street level, step up through the working and sleeping storey towards the light to live in the treetops. The fish are in the river, the deer on the terrace.

Die Räume des Gebäudes sortieren sich entsprechend ihrer Öffentlichkeit. Von der Mitte ausgehend werden die Räume zunehmend privater, an den Enden des Hauses sind sie fast intim. Unterschiedlich stark perforierte Fassadenelemente sind Grundlage der Differenzierung. Ein eingeschossiges Gebäude, 140 Meter lang in der flachen und weiten Schotterebene des Münchener Nordens.

The rooms of this building have been sorted according to their degree of privacy. Starting in the middle, the rooms become more private towards the outside; at the ends they are almost intimate. Varying perforations in the facade elements are responsible for these differences. Single-storied, measuring 140 metres in length and located on the stony planes north of Munich.

Der alte Sportplatz am Ortsende von Schondorf wird schon lange nicht mehr bespielt. Ein neues Sportzentrum hat ihn abgelöst und die Gemeinde hat das Grundstück über einen Investorenwettbewerb gewinnbringend verkauft. Unser Vorschlag sah eine Streusiedlung von Einzelhäusern vor, landschaftlich gebettet in die Endmoräne.

The old sports ground on the outskirts of Schondorf has not been used for many years. It has been replaced by a new sports centre, and the community has sold the plot at a profit within the framework of an investor competition. Our scheme proposed a scattered arrangement of single-family dwellings embedded in the landscape of the end moraine.

>278 >697

412
NEUE STADTHALLE BRUDERHAUSGELÄNDE
New town hall Bruderhaus area

2008
Reutlingen
106.549 cbm
Wettbewerb Ankauf | competition purchase
Große Kreisstadt Reutlingen
LPH 1-2 G/F

>284 >698

031
HAUS H
House H

2005
Stockdorf
1.139 cbm
fertiggestellt | completed
privat | private
LPH 1-8 G/F/A

032
HAUS M
House M

2005
Inning
1.139 cbm
Studie | study
privat | private
LPH 1-2 G/F/A

>296 >699

033
HAUS MV
House MV

2006
Feldafing
1.033 cbm
fertiggestellt | completed
privat | private
LPH 1-8 G/F/A

034
HAUS H2
House H2

2005
Stockdorf
3.691 cbm
fertiggestellt | completed
privat | private
LPH 1-5 G/F/A

>306 >700

035
BÜRO
Office

2005
Greifenberg
691 cbm
fertiggetellt | completed
Forstgut Greifenberg
LPH 1-8 G/F/A

Das ganze Haus kann Veranstaltungsort werden. Foyers und Säle werden variabel zusammengeschaltet. Der Ort kann bis hin zum durchgängig verknüpften Großraum bespielt werden. Raumhohe Vorhänge zwischen den Glashüllen schützen die Foyerbereiche bei Bedarf vor Sonne und Blicken oder unterteilen im Inneren die Räume.
The whole building can become a venue. The foyers and halls can be connected in different ways. It is possible to create a single large space by linking all the individual rooms. Room-high curtains integrated between the two glass skins protect the foyer from the sun and prevent passers-by looking in; the curtains can also be used to separate rooms inside.

Die beiden großen Kiefern auf dem Grundstück wollten wir erhalten. Das Gebäude knickt sich um die Bäume und formt den Eingangsbereich. Der Knick deformiert das nach Bauvorschrift geforderte Walmdach. Ein etwas skurriler Dachraum entstand, im Inneren sichtbar in Beton geschalt. Sägerau, wie auch die Außenverschalung des Hauses.
Our aim was to preserve the two large pines. The building now zigzags around the trees creating an entrance area. The sharp bend distorts the hipped roof requested by the building authorities. The outcome is a slightly bizarre roof, which has been cast in concrete, the traces of the shuttering visible on the inside – raw-sawn timber, like the sheathing on the outside of the house.

Das bayerische Fernsehn nannte es „Fernrohr". Ein etwas sperriger Begriff für ein Haus. Vielleicht, weil es sich förmlich zwischen die Umgebung schiebt und den Blick fokusiert wie eine Röhre. Ein Haus für zwei Personen auf einem sehr schmalen Grundstück. Mit eigentlich nur einem Raum.
The Bavarian television called it a telescope. A slightly awkward term for a building. However, perhaps due to the fact that it "telescopes" into its surroundings and, like a tube, focuses on the view. A house for two people on a very narrow plot with really only one room.

Für unser Büro wurden die Räumlichkeiten in der Försterei des Schlosses zu eng und wir bekamen die Möglichkeit, gegenüber in den ehemaligen Zehentstadel, den „Soldatenspeicher" zu ziehen. Mit einem knappen Budget dämmten wir die Raumhülle, bauten eine einfache Heizung ein und fertigten die Einrichtung aus lackierten Stahlblechtafeln. Alles Übrige beließen wir wie es war.
We were running out of space in the former forester's house at the manor and were given the opportunity to move into the former Zehentstadel, which was once a soldiers' barn. With little to spend, we insulated the shell, installed a simple heating system and fitted it out with varnished sheet steel panels. We left everything else as it was.

413
FINANZAMT GARMISCH - PARTENKIRCHEN
Garmisch - Partenkirchen tax office

2007
Garmisch - Partenkirchen
25.300 cbm
Wettbewerb | competition
Staatliches Bauamt Weilheim
LPH. 1-2 G/F

>316 >701 **036**
HAUS B
House B

2005
Schondorf
2.489 cbm
Studie | study
privat | private
LPH 1-4 G/F/A

>320 >702 **037.1**
FREMDENVERKEHRSAMT LANDSBERG
Landsberg am Lech tourist office

2008
Landsberg
626 cbm
fertiggestellt Wettbewerb 1.Preis | completed competition 1.price
Stadt Landsberg | city Landsberg
LPH 1-5 G/F/A

>330 >703 **037.2**
RATHAUS LANDSBERG AM LECH
Landsberg am Lech city council

2009
Landsberg
4.300 cbm
im bau Wettbewerb 1.Preis | in construction 1.price
Stadt Landsberg | city Landsberg
LPH 1-5 G/F/A

414
PUNKTHÄUSER IN KAUFBEUREN
Kaufbeuren dot houses

2008
Kaufbeuren
13.800 cbm
Wettbewerb | competition
Kreis- und Stadtsparkasse Kaufbeuren
LPH. 1-2 G/F

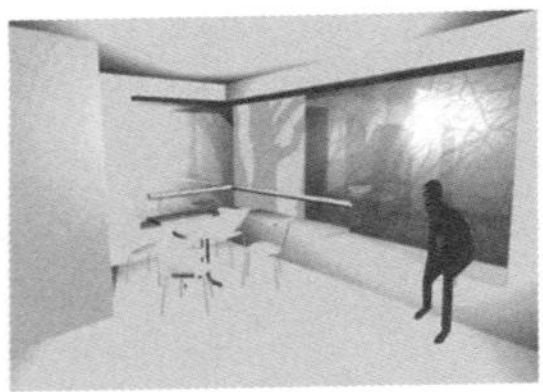

>352 >704 **038**
HAUS H3
House H3

2009
Schondorf
998 cbm
im bau | in constuction
privat | private
LPH 1-8 G/F/A

Eine elegante und moderne Villa sollte es werden. Beeindruckt waren wir von der kürzlich erworbenen Yacht der Bauherren. Zwei Menschen, zwei Hunde und zwei Autos sollten sich hier wohlfühlen. Mit Blick über den See, mit üppigem Zwinger für die Hunde und mit Autostellplatz im Wellnessbereich sollte jeder auf seine Kosten kommen.
The aim was to create an elegant and modern mansion. We were very impressed by the yacht the clients had only recently purchased. Two people, two dogs and two cars were to feel at home. With a view across the lake, a large kennel for the dogs and parking in the spa, everybody's needs were met.

Das historische Rathaus in Landsberg am Lech wurde 1765 von Dominikus Zimmermann erbaut. In einem eingeladenen Wettbewerb suchte die Stadt nach Lösungen zur Erweiterungen des Baudenkmals. Der historische Sitzungssaal war zu klein geworden und eine behindertengerechte Erschließung und ein zweiter Rettungsweg aus dem Altbau fehlten. Unser Beitrag konnte sich durchsetzen. Wir verlegten das Fremdenverkehrsamt aus der Mitte des Altbaus in die nördliche Gewölbeachse und konnten so die historische Durchfahrt in den Hinterhof wieder öffnen.
The historical town hall in Landsberg am Lech was built by Dominikus Zimmermann in 1765. A small invited competition was initiated to look for a solution to extend the listed building. The original council chamber had become too small, and the old building lacked access for disabled people and a second escape route. Our design was accepted. We moved the tourist office from the centre of the old building into the northern vaults and were therefore able to reopen the ancient archway to the rear courtyard.

Den neuen Ratssaal entwickelten wir im Obergeschoß und stellten das Erdgeschoß überwiegend frei. Mit neuem Foyer und Gastronomiebereich entstand eine neue attraktive Querverbindung in der historischen Altstadt und Belebung der Brachflächen. Komplett umhüllt mit einem leichten Kupfergewebe tritt der Neubau in Kontakt mit dem barocken Bestand. Gefiltertes Licht lässt im Inneren eine seriöse Sitzungsatmosphäre entstehen.
We planned the new council chamber on the first floor and kept the ground floor as clear as possible. A new entrance hall and dining area have created a new attractive link in the historical old town and revitalised derelict land. Totally enveloped with a light mesh of copper, the extension harmonises well with the original Baroque building. Filtered light helps to convey a dignified atmosphere in the council chamber.

Die Eltern gaben den Gartenteil am Seeweg an die Familie der Tochter. Die Uferbebauung gegenüber öffnet sich an dieser Stelle für einen Blickbezug über den See. Über ein 2-geschossiges Panoramafenster fasst das Haus präzise diese Aussicht.
The parents gave the garden part of their plot on Seeweg to their daughter's family. Due to the large gap between the buildings opposite, the lake is clearly visible. A two-storey panoramic window focuses precisely on this view.

>364 >705

039
HAUS F
House F

2007
Gräfelfing
2.301 cbm
fertiggestellt | completed
privat | private
LPH. 1-8 G/F/A

>378 >706

415
STADTMUSEUM KAUFBEUREN
Kaufbeuren town museum

2007
Kaufbeuren
3.803 cbm
Wettbewerb | competition
Stadt Kaufbeuren
LPH. 1-2 G/F

>386 >707

040
HAUS S
House S

2007
Berg
1.826 cbm
fertiggestellt | completed
privat | private
LPH 1-8 G/F/A

>394 >708

041
HAUS K2
House K2

2006
Gauting
895 cbm
fertiggestellt | completed
privat | private
LPH 1-8 G/F/A

042
HAUS K3
House K3

2008
Diessen
980 cbm
fertiggestellt | completed
privat | private
LPH 1-8 G

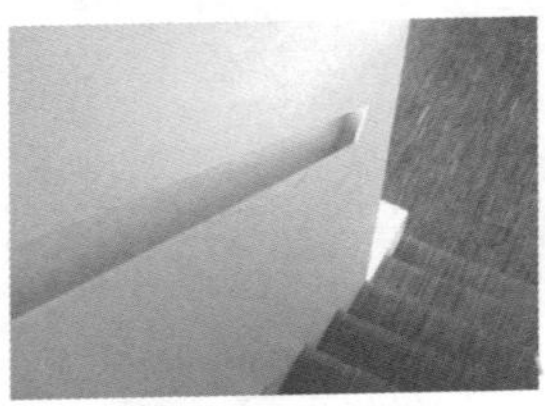

416
WOHNUNGSBAU IN ANSBACH
Ansbach residential area

2009
Ansbach
24.400 cbm
Wettbewerb engere Wahl | competition shortlist
Joseph - Stiftung, Bamberg
LPH. 1-2 G/F

Ein Haus für eine Familie. An jeder Ecke des Grundstückes ein alter Baum, zugeordnet geputzte Kuben für die Privaträume der Obergeschosse. Großzügig in Winkelform verbunden im Erdgeschoß. Hier isst, kocht und liest man gemeinsam. Fast eine kleine Siedlung ist entstanden, die dem Wachsen und Schrumpfen der Familie gerecht wird.

A house for a family. A mature tree in each corner of the plot; assigned to these, rendered cubes for the private rooms on the first floor, which are generously connected by an L-shaped structure in the ground floor. This is where the family eats, cooks and reads together. It's almost like a small housing estate that can adapt to the family's needs for more or less space.

Das neue Eingangsgebäude zum Stadtmuseum reiht sich mit seinen geneigten Flächen selbstverständlich in die giebel- und traufständigen Gebäude der Gasse ein. Der Erweiterungsbau füllt die rückwärtigen Hofbereiche auf, so wie es das Baurecht erlaubt. Eine neue einläufige Treppe erschließt die Ausstellung. Gefiltertes Licht war uns ein Anliegen.

The new entrance building to the town museum, with its sloped surfaces, is well integrated in the gable and saddled roof landscape of the alleyway. As is permitted by the building code, the extension fills the gaps in the rear courtyard. A new single-flight staircase offers access to the exhibition. We specifically planned filtered light.

Historische Villengrundstücke in See naher Lage werden von den Erben häufig geteilt und parkähnliche Wohngegenden mithin nachverdichtet. Der zur Verfügung stehende Bauraum wird durch alte Baulinien, Abstandsflächen und nachbarschaftliche Vereinbarungen bestimmt. Das vorgeschriebene Satteldach darübergelegt, Carport und Haus eingezogen, ergab sich die Form.

Former large estates on the banks of the lake are often divided by the heirs and, as a result, parkland estates are being densified. The actual construction space is defined by old building lines, distance space and neighbourhood arrangements. The shape is the result of setting the requested saddle roof on top and integrating carport and living areas.

Das eigentlich zum Kauf vorgesehene Grundstück war teuer und baurechtlich sehr eingeschränkt. Nach genauer Analyse fühlte man sich der nahegelegenen „Teppichsiedlung“ der 60er Jahre verbunden. Hier war noch eine Parzelle frei und günstig zu erwerben. Mit vorgeschriebener Bungalowbebauung und strikten Vorschriften zum Innenhof. Die Bauherren entschieden sich, und so ist unter strengen wirtschaftlichen Vorgaben das letzte Haus der Siedlung erst jetzt entstanden.

The plot, which had first been considered, proved too expensive and was very restricted from a building regulations point of view. After careful analysis, the clients actually felt far more at home in the 60's residential area nearby with its carpet pattern coverage. There was a single undeveloped plot for sale. Despite the tight regulations, only allowing a bungalow with an atrium courtyard. Notwithstanding the very tight budget, the last house in this residential area has just been completed.

>406 >709

043
HAUS U
House U

2007
Riederau
1.320 cbm
fertiggestellt | completed
privat | private
LPH 1-8 G/F/A

>416 >710

044
SPARKASSE MIT REIHENHÄUSERN
Sparkasse branch office with terraced houses

2006
Landsberg
15.590 cbm
in Planung | intended
Sparkasse Landsberg
LPH 1-5 G/F/A

>428 >711

045
HAUS B2
House B2

2008
Obermenzing
1.468 cbm
fertiggestellt | completed
privat | private
LPH 1-8 G/F/A

046
SIP SCOOTERSHOP
SIP Scootershop

2007
Landsberg
4.300 cbm
fertiggestellt | completed
SIP Scootershop
LPH 1-8 G/F/A

047
HAUS Y
House Y

2006
Stockdorf
1.620 cbm
Studie | study
privat | private
LPH 1-2 G

048
HAUS W3
House W3

2007
Obermenzing
1.406 cbm
fertiggestellt | completed
privat | private
LPH 1-8 G

Kollegen hatten schon versucht, den Wunsch eines älteren Ehepaares, nach einem Haus im klassisch modernen Stil mit Flachdach zu verwirklichen. Die Gemeinde wollte dies auf keinen Fall, da der Bebauungsplan Satteldächer vorsah. So entstand unser Konzept in freier Umsetzung der Regeln. Die Assoziationen mit den Themen des nahen Sees gefielen den Bauherren. Tiefe Dachüberstände schützen nun die großen Verglasungen zum See hin, während sich die andere Seite zur angrenzenden Bahnlinie schließt.
Colleagues had already tried to fulfil the client's dream of a house in a modern classic style with a flat roof. However, the building authority wouldn't grant planning permission since the development plan only permitted saddle roofs. This is where our free interpretation of the rules came. The elderly couple liked our way of dealing with the nearby lake. Extensive roof overhangs protect the fully glazed walls looking out onto the lake, whereas the opposite side, facing the train tracks, is closed.

Die Sparkasse Landsberg am Lech hat für ihre Geschäftsstelle am Eingang der Stadt einen Wettbewerb ausgelobt. Unser Beitrag sollte die städtebauliche Situation stärken. Zusammen mit dem Giebel des gegenüberliegenden Klosters wird der Raum gefasst. Ein Knick in der Fassade, entlang der Münchner Straße, verstärkt diese Wirkung. Viergeschossige Reihenhäuser im rückwärtigen Bereich ergänzen die Anlage.
The bank, Sparkasse Landsberg, initiated a competition for their branch on the route into Landsberg am Lech. The aim of our contribution was to emphasise the entrance into town. Together with the gable of the monastery opposite, the space is framed. A kink in the facade along Munich Street reinforces this effect. Four-storey terraced houses to the rear form part of the development.

Im Münchner Westen ändern sich die Strukturen. Langfristige Erbpachtverträge laufen aus und die Grundstücke werden neu verteilt. Die Lage ist Stadt nah und gerade von jungen Familien begehrt. Ein strenger Bebauungsplan soll die 100jährige Idylle retten.
The structures are changing in the western parts of Munich. Long-term leaseholds are expiring and the plots are changing hands. The location is close to town and especially attractive for young families. A strict development plan is trying to save the 100-year-old idyllic character.

>436 >712

417
MEISTERHÄUSER DESSAU
Dessau Masters' Houses

2008
Dessau
3.060 cbm
Wettbewerb | competition in collaboration with Anne Beer
Jost Consult Projektsteuerungs GmbH
LPH. 1-2 G/F

049
UMBAU HÜHNERSTALL
Hen house refurbishment

2007
Inning
462 cbm
fertiggestellt | completed
privat | private
LPH 1-8 A

050
VERWALTUNGSERWEITERUNG SYNCHRO
Extension of Syncro headquarters

2004
Schongau
3.560 cbm
Studie | study
privat | private
LPH 1-3 G

>442 >713

051
UMBAU DATSCHA
Dacha refurbishment

2004
Holzhausen
189 cbm
fertiggestellt | completed
privat | private
LPH 1-8 G/A

>448 >714

418
SEEANLAGEN DIESSEN
Diessen lake complex

2008
Diessen
7.850 cbm
Wettbewerb | competition
Marktgemeinde Diessen am Ammersee
LPH. 1-2 G/F

052
HAUS F2
House F2

2008
Herrsching
1.950 cbm
fertiggestellt | completed
privat | private
LPH 1-8 G/F/A

Über einen Wettbewerb sollten die zerstörten „Meisterhäuser" der historischen Bauhaussiedlung in Dessau wiederhergestellt werden. Der Preisträger interpretierte die weißen Kuben der verlorenen Vorgängerbauten im Abguss als schwarze, monolithische Skulpturen. Das war auch unser Ansatz.
Wir interpretierten auch die Öffnungen der Ursprungsbauten. Der Preisträger blieb abstrakt.
A competition was initiated to reconstruct the destroyed Meisterhäuser in the historical Bauhaus-Siedlung in Dessau. The award winner interpreted the white cubes of the historical predecessors by creating replicas as black, monolithic sculptures. This was also our approach. We also interpreted the apertures of the original buildings. The award winner's approach was more abstract.

Eine Hütte mit langer Geschichte. Einst Bootshaus auf Pfählen im See, musste sie wegen großer Eisschübe um 1910 an Land gezogen werden, wanderte über die Jahre hoch an die jetzige Stelle und gab in den Münchner Bombennächten des 2. Weltkrieges der Familie Unterschlupf. Man hing an der Hütte. Und da auch nicht jeder Schritt der Baugeschichte behördlich angezeigt wurde, kam nur eine Sanierung in Frage: Neuer Innenausbau, eine großzügige Befensterung und Schiebeläden für jene Tage, an denen man die kleine Datscha nicht nutzt.
A cottage with a long story. Once a boathouse on piles in the lake, it had to be pulled up onto land due to incredible ice formations in 1910. Over the years, it moved up the slope to where it stands today and provided the family with shelter during the Munich bombings in the Second World War. The cottage is cherished. Because not every step during the long history of the house has been registered by the authorities, it was only possible to perform refurbishments: A new interior, generous window formats and movable shutters for the days when the cottage is not being used.

Schon lange gab es den Wunsch, die Seeanlagen von Dießen am Ammersee neu zu ordnen. Nun wurde ein offener Wettbewerb gewagt. Aus der vorgefundenen Topografie entwickelten wir eine Struktur von Schollen und Kanten. Raumbildend und in Teilen für geforderte Funktionen raumhaltig.
The desire to reorganise Dießen's lake complex at Lake Ammersee has been in the pipeline for a long time. When an opportunity presented, an open competition was initiated. Based on the topography, we developed a structure of slabs and ridges. Space creating and in part also space accommodating to house the requested functions.

053
INSTANDSETZUNG DATSCHA
Dacha refurbishment

2006
Herrsching
254 cbm
im bau | in construction
privat | private
LPH 1-3 G

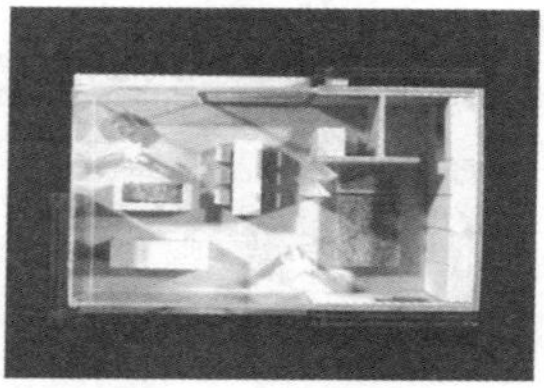

054
HAUSPAAR
Twin dwellings

2008
Inning
1.559/1.577 cbm
fertiggestellt | completed
privat | private
LPH 4-8 G

055
HAUS A
House A

2006
Gröbenzell
1.164 cbm
Studie | study
privat | private
LPH 1-2 G

>456 >715
056
HAUS D
House D

2008
bei München
o. A.
fertiggestellt | completed
privat | private
LPH 1-8 G/F/A

>470 >716
057
HAUS S2
House S2

2008
Breitbrunn
1.934 cbm
fertiggestellt | completed
privat | private
LPH 1-8 G/F/A

>486 >717
419
REALSCHULE KAUFERING
Kaufering secondary school

2008
Kaufering
7.100 cbm
Wettbewerb 2.Preis | competition 2.price
Landkreis Landsberg am Lech
LPH. 1-2 G/F

Ein Haus, südlich von München, in einem seit 100 Jahren gewachsenen Villenvorort. Das Grundstück war großzügig und man konnte sich in die Fläche entwickeln. Transparent im Erdgeschoss mit einem weit auskragenden Obergeschoss. Der Blick in den eigenen Garten fokussiert, die Nachbarn ausgeblendet. Das Obergeschoss eine weiße Röhre mit Satteldach, umgesetzt ohne störende Verblechung, bündig eingedeckt mit weißem Faserzement.
A house, south of Munich, in a traditionally grown, 100-year-old garden suburb. The plot was large and it was possible to spread out. A totally transparent ground floor with a clearly protruding upper level. The view is focussed on the garden, not the neighbours. The upper storey is a simple white tube with a saddle roof built without disturbing flashings and a flush roof covering made of white fibrous concrete.

Ein Grundstück, nach dem man suchen muss, mit einem Bebauungsplan, der dann aber wenig Freiraum lässt. Kleine Maßnahmen müssen ausreichen, um zu entkommen. Das wenig verzogene Walmdach, der leicht geknickte Hauptbaukörper, eine Verbindung von Garage und Haupthaus.
A plot, one difficult to find, and a development plan with little leeway. This is where small features have to suffice. A slightly distorted hipped roof, a slightly kinked main structure, a link between the garage and the main structure.

Wir wollten eine kompakte Schule. Das übergroße Grundstück sollte damit für zukünftige Entwicklungen flexibel bleiben. Ein wirtschaftlicher Schulbau mit dennoch differenzierten räumlichen Qualitäten. Mehrere Innenhöfe. Viel Licht, von allen Seiten. Eine große, multifunktionale Freitreppe im zentralen Foyer.
We wanted a compact school. Our aim was to leave space on the overly large plot for further developments. An economical school building with nevertheless differentiated spatial qualities. Several courtyards, and light from all angles. A wide multi-functional flight of stairs in the central entrance hall.

>490 >718

058
HAUS R
House R

2009
Schondorf
2.800 cbm
im bau | in construction
privat | private
LPH 1-8 G/F/A

059
ERWEITERUNG EINES WOHNHAUSES
House extension

2007
Gröbenzell
128 cbm
fertiggestellt | completed
privat | private
LPH 1-4 G

>512 >719

420
BÜRGER - UND KULTURZENTRUM ALTÖTTING
Altötting cultural and community centre

2008
Altötting
29.600 cbm
Wettbewerb 4.Preis | competition 4.price
Stadt Altötting
LPH. 1-2 G/F

060
ACKERMANNBOGEN MÜNCHEN
Munich Ackermannbogen

2008
München - Neuhausen
12.150 cbm
in Planung | intended
Bau Zeit
LPH 1-2 G/F

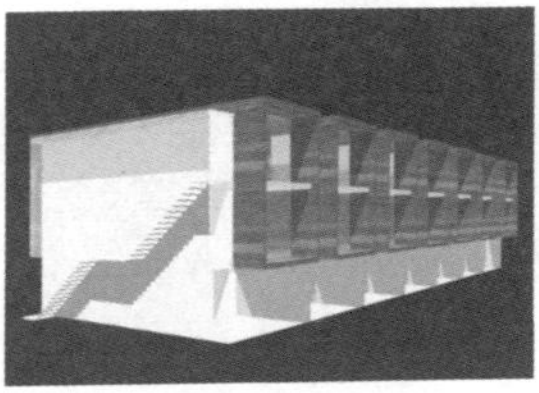

061
HAUS V
House V

2006
Wartaweil
3.200 cbm
Studie | study
privat | private
LPH 1-2 G

062
WOHNUNGSUMBAU
Apartment conversion

2006
München-Schwabing
456 cbm
fertiggestellt | completed
privat | private
LPH 1-8 G

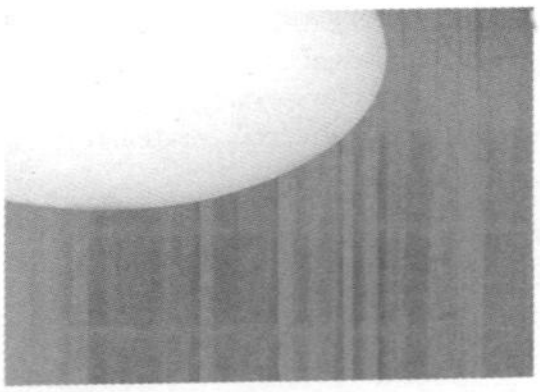

Schondorf am Ammersee, mit guter örtlicher Infrastruktur, der Nähe zur Münchner Innenstadt einerseits und zum Flughafen andererseits, wird als Wohnort stark nachgefragt. Eine Villa für ein unternehmerisches Paar mit Gestaltungskompetenz, Neugier und Mut. Ein Haus mit komplexen Funktionsabläufen. Ein skulptural gefasster Landschaftsblick. 380 massive Acrylglaszylinder perforieren die Gebäudeaußenwand.
Schondorf on Lake Ammersee has become an attractive place to live due its location, its good infrastructure, the short distance to Munich and the airport. A mansion for a business couple, curious, brave and interested in design. A house with complex functional sequences. A framed view of the sculptural landscape. 380 massive acrylic glass cylinders perforating the building's exterior skin.

Ein neues Bürger- und Kulturzentrum für Altötting, einen bedeutenden Wahlfahrtsort in Bayern. Das Grundstück im Übergangsbereich von dicht bebauter Altstadt und offener Bebauung, zwischen Hauptplatz mit Wallfahrtskirche und solitärem Bau des „Panoramas" auf der Obstwiese. Wir sahen an dieser Stelle in der Raumfolge der Stadt und als Zäsur zur historischer Altstadt einen städtischen Platz mit öffentlichen Funktionen.
A new community and cultural centre for Altötting, possibly the most renowned place of pilgrimage in Bavaria. The plot on the border between the dense old town and more open structures, between the main square with the pilgrimage church and the solitary, circular Panorama building in the fruit orchard. Our design envisioned an urban square with community facilities to fit into the sequence of urban space and as a transition point to the historical old town.

063
FUSSBALL STUTTGART
Football Stuttgart

2007
Stuttgart
11 cbm
fertiggestellt | completed
privat | private
LPH 1

>518 >720

064
DEUTSCHES PATENT- UND MARKENAMT
German Patent and Trade Mark Office

2009
München
7.114 cbm
im bau | in construction
Deutsches Patentamt | german Patent office
LPH 1-8 G/A

065
HAUS S3
House S3

2006
Feldafing
3.200 cbm
Studie | study
privat | private
LPH 1-2 G

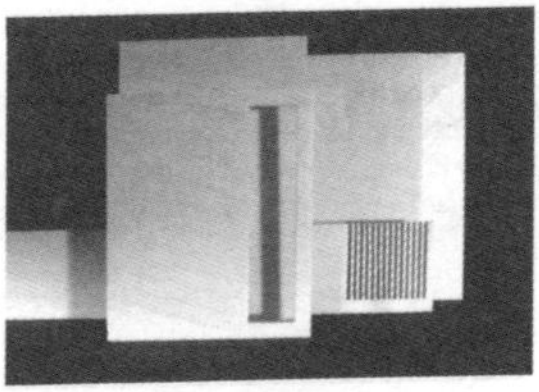

>536 >721

066
HAUS N
House N

2009
Bachern
2.176 cbm
im bau | in construction
privat | private
LPH 1-8 G/F/A

>550 >722

421
JUGENDHAUS NEUGABLONZ
Neugablonz youth centre

2008
Kaufbeuren-Neugablonz
3.770 cbm
Wettbewerb | competition
Stadt Kaufbeuren
LPH. 1-2 G/F

422
SOS KINDERDORF DIESSEN
Diessen SOS children's village

2009
Diessen
2.268 cbm
Wettbewerb | competition
SOS Kinderdorf e.V.
LPH. 1-2 G/F

Mit der Digitalisierung von Patenten wurde die Auslegehalle des Deutschen Patent- und Markenamtes (DPMA) nur noch wenig als kleiner Veranstaltungsraum genutzt. Man entschloss sich, den Raum wieder wachzurütteln als großen Veranstaltungs- und Konferenzraum. Die große Geste der Stahlbetonkassettendecke aus der Erbauungszeit war noch vorhanden, die ursprünglich umlaufenden Holzeinbauten abhanden gekommen. Diese Elemente wurden wieder hergestellt und in ihrer Erscheinung geschärft. Entmaterialisiert ergänzt und transluzent hinterleuchtet die räumliche Umhüllung.
Since the digitalisation of patent records, the patent presentation hall of the German Patent and Trade Mark Office (DPMA) has been used only occasionally as a small function room. A decision was made to reinvigorate the space as a large function and conference room. The remarkable reinforced concrete waffle ceiling from the original construction was still in place; the surrounding wooden panelling no longer. These elements were carefully reinstated and their appearance enhanced. Everything else was added in a dematerialised manner and the translucent spatial enclosure was backlit.

Es durfte ein Haus aus Beton werden, dabei atmosphärisch und nicht zu nüchtern. Das Grundstück war steil und schmal, die Aussicht in Teilen spektakulär. Weitauskragende Balkonbügel stellen exklusive Blickbezüge frei und blenden Umfeld aus. Das reduzierte Materialkonzept setzt auf Sichtbeton und dunkles Eloxal.
It was allowed to be made of concrete, however, with a pleasant atmosphere and not too cold. The plot was steep and narrow, with spectacular views. Far protruding balconies function as excellent lookouts and blend out the surroundings. The material concept is basic and focuses on exposed concrete and dark eloxal.

Ein Jugendhaus für Neugablonz musste sich- räumlich speziell- um den Sportplatz organisieren und mit der umgebenden Siedlungsstruktur der 50er auseinandersetzen. Wir dachten an eine dynamische Geste mit Bezug zur angrenzenden Straßenkreuzung und Motive von Pavillonbauten dieser Zeit. Ein geschwungenes Gebäude mit überdachtem Zugangsplatz in der Mitte.
Especially from a spatial point of view, the youth centre in Neugablonz had to be arranged around the sports field and compete with the 50's architecture of the surroundings. We envisioned a dynamic shape in correspondence to the nearby crossroad and features reminiscent of pavilions from this era. A curved building with a covered square in the centre.

>556 >723

067
HAUS V2
House V2

2007
Unterbachern
1.100 cbm
Studie | study
privat | private
LPH 1-2 G

068
HAUS P
House P

2007
Wartaweil
3.748 cbm
Studie | study
privat | private
LPH 1-2 G

>560 >724

423
STÄDTEBAU „AUBING - OST"
Urban planning „Aubing - Ost"

2008
München Aubing
112.100 cbm
Wettbewerb | competition
aurelis Real Estate GmbH & Co. KG
LPH. 1-2 G/F

>568 >725

069
HAUS J
House J

2009
Landsberg
1.967 cbm
im bau | in construction
privat | private
LPH 1-8 G/F/A

070
HAUS B3
House B3

2007
Gmund
2.016 cbm
Studie | study
privat | private
LPH 1-2 G

424
GESUNDHEITSZENTRUM AUGSBURG
Augsburg health centre

2009
Augsburg
19.100 cbm
Wettbewerb | competition
Kongregation der Barmherzigen Schwestern
LPH. 1-2 G/F

Die Bauherrin war mutig, das Gebäude auch. Das Gebäude angehoben, um darunter zu parken, und ausgehölt zu nur einem Raum blieb das Haus in seiner Form der Umgebung sehr ähnlich, im Wesentlichen war es anders. Sehr anders und so sehr anders, dass es, zumindest bisher, noch nicht gebaut wurde.
The client was brave and so was the building. Raised to provide parking underneath and hollowed out leaving only one room. Like this it was in unison with the environment, but actually also quite different. So different that it hasn't been built, at least not yet.

Die erforderlichen Mindestabstandsflächen zu Nachbargebäuden entsprechend Baurecht erzeugen häufig schlecht nutzbare, wenig qualitätsvolle Zwischenräume mit sogenanntem Abstandsgrün. Die Teppichsiedlungen der 60er und 70er Jahre umgingen über Bebauungspläne mit direkter Grenzbebauung diese Abhängigkeit. Die kompakte Organisationsform ergab bei geringem Landverbrauch hochwertige halböffentliche Erschließungsbereiche und gut geschnittene private Hofgärten. Hier wollten wir anknüpfen.
Standard building regulations define the distance to be maintained between neighbouring plots. The leftover space, the so-called green strip, is frequently limited in use and lacks quality. Developments with carpet coverage, which emerged in the 60's and 70's, avoided this conflict by planning patio houses set on the boundaries. These dense and compact estates with low levels of land consumption offer high-quality semi-private access areas and fair sized atrium gardens. These are the features we wanted to revive.

Ordentliche Giebelhäuser entlang des neuen Angers, das war das Konzept des Bebauungsplanes. Das Grundstück war tief und die Bauherren nicht unbedingt konventionell. Ein eher freies Wohnen wurde bevorzugt.
Tidy gable houses alongside the new meadow – this was the concept of the development plan. On top of this, the plot was deep and the clients not necessarily conventional. The preference was for a more free-style way of living.

>586 >726 **071**
HAUS D2
House D2

2009
Diessen
2.526 cbm
im bau | in construction
privat | private
LPH 1-4 G/F

425
ASAMGEBÄUDE DOMBERGAUFGANG
Asam building access to cathedral

2009
Freising
17.435 cbm
Wettbewerb Ankauf | competition puchase
Stadt Freising
LPH. 1-2 G/F

426
DREIFACHSPORTHALLE UHLANDSCHULE
Nuremberg sports hall Uhland school

2009
Nürnberg
23.153 cbm
Wettbewerb | competition
Stadt Nürnberg
LPH. 1-2 G/F

072
HAUS F3
House F3

2007
Schondorf
859 cbm
Studie | study
privat | private
LPH 1-4 G

073
HAUS SZ
House SZ

2008
Starnberg
2.176 cbm
studie | study
privat | private
LPH 1-8 G/F/A

>590 >727 **074**
HAUS BN
House BN

2009
Buch
1.300 cbm
im bau | in contruction
privat | private
LPH 1-8 G

Der Bauherr, Inhaber einer Schreinerei für den gehobenen Innenausbau, ist selbst Planer. Unsere Aufgabe war es, seine Skizzen und Entwürfe zu ordnen und in Form zu bringen. Das Gebäude erscheint nun innen wie außen weiß in weiß, obwohl doch durch und durch in Holz konstruiert. Milimetergenau gefügt, wie es einem Schreiner lieb ist. Statt Blechen und Aluminiumprofilen wurde acrylgebundener Mineralwerkstoff verwendet. Das Haus soll als Musterhaus für ein neues Label von innovativen Fertighäusern dienen.

The client, the owner of a joinery shop for upmarket finishes, is in actual fact a planner himself. It was our job to sort through his sketches and designs and give them form. From inside and outside the building appears totally white, despite being made of wood and nothing but wood. Accurate down to the very last millimetre, as one would expect of a joiner. Acrylic-bound mineral materials were used instead of sheet metal and aluminium flashings. The house is a show house for a new line of innovative prefab homes.

Wieder sollte im Garten eines Landhauses ein Neubau entstehen. Ein Haus für zwei Menschen, mit zwei großen Einschnitten belichtet und dem Auto unter dem Haus.

Once again, we were commissioned to plan a new home in the garden of a country estate. A house for two people with daylight entering through two large incision-like openings and the car parked below the house.

427
SCHULHAUS MÜHLEMATT
Mühlematt school building

2009
Mühlematt
11.155 cbm
Wettbewerb | competition
Stadt Lenzburg
LPH. 1-2 G/F

>600 >728
075
HAUS E2
House E2

2009
Inning
1.252 cbm
im bau | in construction
privat | private
LPH 1-8 G/F/A

076
HAUS K4
House K4

2009
München - Fasanerie
1.696 cbm
im bau | in construction
privat | private
LPH. 1-8 G/F/A

428
STUDENTENWOHNHEIM COBURG
Coburg student dormitory

2009
Koburg
7.620 cbm
Wettbewerb | competition
Studentenwerk Oberfranken
LPH. 1-2 G/F

429
UNI HOMBURG
Uni Homburg

2009
Homburg
34.069 cbm
Wettbewerb | competition
Saarland
LPH. 1-2 G/F

>610 >729
077
HAUS V3
House V3

2009
Hechendorf
2.100 cbm
im bau | in construction
privat | private
LPH 1-8 G/F/A

Ein flacher Nordhang am Ortsrand der kleinen oberbayerischen Gemeinde wurde in den 60er Jahren durch einen Bauträger mit ein und demselben Haustyp bebaut. Die Häuser waren zweistöckig in die abfallende Topografie eingepasst, mit dem Wohnen im oberen Geschoss. So hatte man einen guten Bezug zum oberen, südlichen Garten und einen weiten Blick in die Weite der westlichen Flur. Wir haben den Typus reinterpretiert, wenig angepasst.
In the 60ies, a property developer covered a gentle north-facing slope on the outskirts of a small Upper Bavarian community with identical houses. The dwellings are set into the hillside, two-storied with living areas on the upper floors. The result is good accessibility to the upper, south-facing gardens and wonderful views to the western planes. We have reinterpreted this type of living; not a lot resembles the original.

Ein erster Entwurf stand bereits, da änderten sich Bauplatz und See. Alle Bemühungen, den quadratischen Flachbau in die neue Situation zu implantieren, funktionierten nicht recht. Das neue Grundstück verlangte nach einem landschaftlicheren Konzept.
A first design had been completed, then the plot changed, including the lake. All efforts to implant the square flat roofed building into the new situation were in vain. The new plot required a landscaped concept.

>622 >730

078
LANDHAUS
Cottage

2009
Unterallgäu
2.045 cbm
im bau | in construction
privat | private
LPH 1-8 G/F/A

079
HAUS P2
House P2

2008
Diessen
1.100 cbm
Studie | study
privat | private
LPH 1-2 G

>642 >731

430
HOTELANLAGE NÜRNBERG
Nuremberg hotel complex

2008
Nürnberg
121.400 cbm
Wettbewerb | competition
wbg Nürnberg GmbH
LPH. 1-2 G/F

080
HAUS S4
House S4

2009
Wörthsee
1.468 cbm
im bau | in construction
privat | private
LPH 1-8 G

081
HAUS G2
House G2

2007
Unterbachern
1.100 cbm
Studie | study
privat | private
LPH 1-4 G

082
HAUS K5
House K5

2009
Pöcking
1.562 cbm
im bau | in construction
privat | private
LPH. 1-8 G/A/F

Ein Gebäude in einer ländlichen Umgebung, bisher landwirtschaftlich geprägt. Mit Wirtschaftsgebäuden in typischer Kubatur und Materialität. In diesen Kontext sollte sich das Gebäude fügen. Mit getrennten Bereichen für privates Wohnen und Gäste.
A building in the countryside, which is mainly used for agriculture. The vernacular buildings all with typical volumes and material concepts. The new house was to blend into this configuration. With separate areas, one to live in and one for guests.

In Verlängerung der „Großen Straße" in Nürnberg, historischer Aufmarschachse des Reichsparteitagsgeländes, sollte ein Hotel mit maximalem Blickbezug zur historischen Altstadt entstehen. Räumlich versetzt zur Strassenachse überragt der Hotelturm den Lärchenwald. Er windet sich ein wenig.
A hotel with a good view of the old town is to be developed at the end of the „Großen Straße", the historical Parade Road of the Party Rally Grounds in Nuremberg. Slightly off axis, the hotel tower reaches well above the larch forest, twisting as it rises.

083
HAUS E3
House E3

2009
Pöcking
1.321 cbm
im bau | in construction
privat | private
LPH 1-8 G/A/F

084
WOHNUNGEN BOGENHAUSEN
Bogenhauesn flats

2008
München Bogenhausen
4.450 cbm
Studie | study
privat | private
LPH. 1 G

>646 >732

085
HAUS S5
House S5

2009
Gräfelfing
1.256 cbm
im bau | in construction
privat | private
LPH 1-8 G/A/F

086
HAUS S6
House S6

2009
Alling
1.683 cbm
in Planung | intended
privat | private
LPH. 1-4 G/F/A

431
ERWEITERUNG SPRENGEL MUSEUM
Sprengel museum extension

2009
Hannover
46.076 cbm
Wettbewerb | competition
Landeshauptstadt Hannover
LPH. 1-2 G/F

432
RATHAUS CRAILSHEIM
Town hall Crailsheim

2009
Crailsheim
7.893 cbm
Wettbewerb | competition
Stadt Crailsheim
LPH. 1-2 G/F

Das Budget war vorgegeben, die Grundrisse vom Bauherren bereits skizziert. Wir haben sie zusammengesetzt, mehr spielerisch, wie gestapelte Boxen.
The budget was fixed, the floor plans already sketched out by the client. We pieced them together in a playful way – staggered like building blocks.

>654 >733

087
GRUNDSCHULE HOLZKIRCHEN
Holzkirchen primary school

2009
Holzkirchen
25.000 cbm
in Planung Wettbewerb 1.Preis | intended competition 1.price
Markt Holzkirchen
LPH. 1-5 G/F

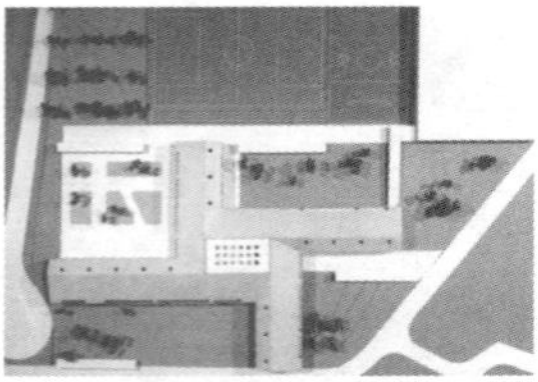

088
RESTAURANT SEEHAUS
Seehaus restaurant

2009
Riederau
254 cbm
in Planung | intended
privat | private
LPH. 1-4 G

>664 >734

089
HAUS E4
House E4

2009
Oberhofen/Irrsee
3.384 cbm
in Planung | intended
privat | private
LPH 1-8 G/F/A

090
HAUS W4
House W4

2009
Gauting
1.808 cbm
in Planung | intended
privat | private
LPH 1-8 G/F/A

091
HAUS E5
House E5

2009
Strasslach
2.106 cbm
in Planung | intended
privat | private
LPH 1-8 G/F/A

092
HAUS G3
House G3

2009
Inning
2.481 cbm
in Planung | intended
privat | private
LPH 1-8 G/F/A

Die bisherige Grundschule war gemeinsam mit der Realschule in einem zeitgenössischen Schulgebäude untergebracht. Die Gemeinde wollte den Zustand ändern. Sie wünschte sich ein eigenes Haus für die Grundschule, eine neue Dorfschule, auch mit Bezug zur Hauslandschaft im Voralpenland. Nicht so betönern, mehr hölzern. Dem Preisgericht hat gefallen, wie „entspannt es den Verfassern gelingt, das große Volumen in die schwierige ortsräumliche Situation einzubinden".

The current primary school is accommodated in the same contemporary school building as the secondary school. The community wanted to change this situation. They really wanted a separate building for the primary school, a village school, which would blend into the roofscape of the alpine upland. Less concrete and more wood. The competition committee liked the way the designers managed to blend the large building volume into the difficult rural situation.

Ein Refugium für Familie und Freunde. Momentan noch Ferienhaus, später vielleicht Altersruhesitz. Man hat uns das Vertrauen gegeben, da wir im 5-Seenland viel gebaut haben und die Gegend hier, hinter Salzburg, vergleichbar ist. Eine idyllische Lage zwischen Bergen und See, im Außenbereich und Landschaftsschutzgebiet. Es gab anspruchsvolle Verhandlungen mit dem Landschaftsschutz.

A hideaway for family and friends. At the moment still a holiday home, later possibly a place to stay when retired. We were commissioned because we had built a lot in the Fünf-Seen-Land (Five-Lakes-District) and the area in this case, behind Salzburg, is comparable. An idyllic place between the mountains and the lake, in its surroundings and the landscape protection area. Challenging negotiations were conducted with authorities concerning landscape protection.

093
SCHUHLAGER
Shoestorage

2009
Greifenberg
784 cbm
In Planung | intended
Primeshoes GmbH
LPH 1-8 G/F/A

>668 >735

433
RATHAUS WETTSTETTEN
Wettstetten town hall

2009
Wettstetten
7.967 cbm
Wettbewerb 1. Preis | competition 1. price
Gemeinde Wettstetten
LPH. 1-2 G/F

094
HAUS M2
House M2

2009
München - Solln
1.520 cbm
In Planung | intended
privat | private
LPH 1-8 G/F/A

095
HAUS H4
House H4

2009
Münsing
1.612 cbm
In Planung | intended
privat | private
LPH 1-8 G/F/A

096
BÜROSANIERUNG DPMA
Patentoffices

2009
München
30.720 cbm
In Planung | intended
Deutsches Patentamt | german Patent office
LPH 1-8 G

097
HAUS H5
House H5

2009
Grünwald
1.517 cbm
In Planung | intended
privat | private
LPH 1-8 G/F/A

Rathaus, Bürgersaal und Altenpflege sollten im Dorfzentrum von Wettstetten neu entstehen. Schon im Vorfeld zum Wettbewerb hatte sich die Gemeinde in Arbeitsgruppen mit der Bauaufgabe auseinandergesetzt. Man wünschte sich einzelne Häuser in Fortschreibung der Körnung des Ortes und seiner Hauslandschaft. Ein nachvollziehbarer Anspruch. Durch die Setzung der Baukörper entstanden unterschiedliche Außenräume eigener Qualität und Funktion, die sich selbstverständlich in das Raumgefüge des Dorfes binden. Ein kleiner Platz in Verknüpfung der Eingangsbereiche, eine schmale Gasse als Wegraum und der große Anger in Zwiesprache mit der Kirche.

The aim was to develop a town hall, a communal hall and a geriatric care centre in the middle of Wettstetten. Before the competition was announced, the community formed teams to discuss the contents of the assignment. They were looking for individual units as a continuation of the fragmented nature of older buildings and its town and roofscape. An understandable approach. Once the various building components were placed, different types and qualities of space emerged for a variety of functions, which naturally blended into the structure of the village. A small place linking the entrances, a narrow path connecting space and a large meadow in a dialogue with the church.

098
PFORTE DPMA
Patententrance

2009
München
705 cbm
In Planung | intended
Deutsches Patentamt | german Patent office
LPH 1-8 G/F/A

434
KLOSTERINSEL RHEINAU
Monastery island Rheinau

2009
Rheinau
89.000 cbm
Wettbewerb 1.Preis | competition 1. price
Baudirektion Kanton Zürich
LPH. 1-2 G/F

Biographien | Biographies Felix Bembé 1969 geboren in München, Deutschland | born in Munich, Germany 1994 Diplom an der Hochschule München | diploma Munich University of Applied Sciences 1999 Bürogründung Bembé Dellinger | Established Bembé Dellinger **Sebastian Dellinger** 1966 geboren in Fürstenfeldbruck, Deutschland | born in Fürstenfeldbruck, Germany 1997 Diplom an der Hochschule München | diploma Munich University of Applied Sciences 1999 Bürogründung Bembé Dellinger | Established Bembé Dellinger

Mitarbeiter | Team members Marion Bruhns, **Arne Bernd**, Tobias Conrad, **Viktor Filimonow**, Alexandra Grad, **Christine Gentsch**, **Gabriel Hägel**, **Johannes Hiller**, Julia Haider, **Sebastian Hoffmann**, **Christoph Johannhörster**, **Christoph Knaus**, Maximilian Krötz, Peter Klass, Steffi Kochbeck, Daniel Maurer, **Björn Manns**, **Carolin Mayer**, Theresa Obermeier, Katharina Pautz, Dominik Poppel, **Vanessa Philipp**, **Martin Riedl**, **Benjamin Saupe**, Alexander Schmidt, **Christian Steinbach**, Jörg Schulte-Wien, Alexander Tochtermann, Torben Tjarks, Lina Winkler, **Gerhard Wohlrab,** Melanie Wildgruber, Tilman Winter, Thomas Wheyrich, Uli Wiese, Roland Zimmerer, Tobias Zimmermann **Modellbau** C. A. Bembé

Auszeichnungen | awards 1999 401 Rudolf Steiner - Schule 2. Preis **2000** Grundschule München-Sendling 3.Preis **2001** Architektouren: 020 Wohnhaus K, **2002** Architektouren: 007 Wohnhaus mit Praxis 1. Wessobrunner Architekturpreis: Preisträger für Wohnen am Ammersee 001 Wohnen im Reiherweg 007 Wohnhaus mit Praxis, 020 Wohnhaus K, 403 Diözesankurie in Rottenburg Ankauf **2003** Architektouren: Wohnbebauung Schraml-Ohrmund in Schondorf am Ammersee, 001 Wohnen im Reiherweg Anerkennung BDA Preis: 003 Atelier im Currypark **2004** Architektouren: 003 Atelier im Currypark, 030,„Alter Sportplatz" in Schondorf 4.Preis **2005** Architektouren: 021 Wohnhaus BL Anerkennung Deubau Preis: 003 Atelier im Currypark Nominierung für den EON Kulturpreis durch die Regierung von Oberbayern allgemein, 405 NRW-Bank in Münster Ankauf, 406 Stadthalle in Penzberg 4. Preis, 407Wohnbebauung Sedanstrasse engere Wahl 037.1 Ratsaal Rathaus Landsberg am Lech 1. Preis, 044 Sparkassengeschäfsstelle mit Reihenhäusern 1.Preis **2006** Architektouren: 013 Wohnbebauung Lachen Birkenalle Nominierung für den EON Kulturpreis durch die Regierung von Oberbayern allgemein, Bayrischer Rundfunk: 032 Wohnhaus M „Traumhäuser", 408 Wohnen und Reiten 1.Preis, 410 Jugendhaus der Verständigung engere Wahl, Europäische Schule in München 3.Preis **2007** Architektouren: 031 Wohnhaus H Bayerischer Wohnungsbaupreis „Neue Nachbarschaften" 013 Wohnbebauung Lachen Birkenalle Schöner Wohnen: „Cleverer Häuser auf kleinem Grund", 2. Preis 013 Wohnbebauung Lachen Birkenalle, 411 Studentenwohnheim in München Freimann engere Wahl **2008** Architektouren: 015 Wohnanlage Gartenstrasse Architektouren: 018 Wohnhaus E Wessobrunner Architekturpreis, Anerkennung: Wohnbebauung Kithier 013 Wohnbebauung Lachen BirkenalleeGrundschule Holzkirchen 1.Preis, Realschule in Kaufering 2.Preis, Neue Stadthalle - Bruderhausgelände in Reutlingen Ankauf, **2009** Architekturjahrbuch 2009/2010 DAM: 013 Wohnbebauung Lachen Birkenallee, 419Bürger - und Kulturzentrum Altötting 4.Preis

Veröffentlichungen | publications 2000 wettbewerbe aktuell 10/00, **2002** 1. Wessobrunner Architekturpreis, 2002 wettbewerbe aktuell 9/02, **2003** 25 Maisons en Bois / Éditions du Moniteur 2003 Bauberater 1/03 Häuser 5/03 AIT 7+8/03 Baumeister 12/03, **2004** Glas-Häuser / DVA, 2004 Bauen auf dem Land / DVA 2004 Interior Digest 1/04 Häuser 1/04Häuser 5/04 AIT 7+8/04 Detail 11+12/04 Bauwelt 13/04 architecture interieure cree, **2005** Architektur Neues Bayern / Verlagshaus Braun 2005PUR! Die neue Schlichtheit anspruchsvoller, Wohnhäuser / DVA 2005, Low Budget / DVA 2005, new kitchen design / daab 2005, new living room design / daab 2005, Case in vetro / Frederico Motta Editore 2005, Baukultur 02/05, Cosina KYXHN /, A & W 5/05, wettbewerbe aktuell 7/05, wettbewerbe aktuell 9/05, Interieure Cree 315 Bayricher Architektur Wettbewerb, 20 Private Wohnträume 04/05, Baukultur 02/05, **2006** Glasbauatlas 2. Auflage / Birkhäuser 2006, Individuelle Küchen / DVA 2006, Salotti d´ autore / Federico Motta Editore 2006, Der Ammersee / Kiebitz Buch 2006, Doppelhäuser und Reihenhäuser / DVA 2006, Neue kleine Häuser / DVA 2006, Der ideale Grundriss 2 / Callwey 2006, Wendel- und Spindeltreppen / DVA 2006, Top 100 Häuser / DVA 2006, Architecture Inspirations / daab 2006, Traumhäuser BR / DVA 2006, Häuser 2/06, Casa Mica 03/06, Häuser 6/06, Focus Nr. 18/06, Garten und Landschaft 9/06, human space furniture 52 / 11/2006, Architektenwettbewerbe in Bayern 2000-2005, Contemporary Houses / Könemann 2006, **2007** i nterior Design, New York 04/2007, Der Weg zum eigenen Haus / Detail pro 2007, Cocinas Diáfanas / Loft 2007, Neue Nachbarschaften Landeswettbewerb Bayr. Wohnungsbaupreis, Dokumentation Wohnbebauung Kithier, Schöner Wohnen 10/2007, A W Special, Häuser 01/2007, Häuser 04/2007, Häuser 06/2007, Das Ideale Einfamilienhaus, Vola Talks 06/2007, AIT 01/01 2007, myself 07/2007, **2008** Wettbewerb Aktuel 03/2008, Wettbewerb Aktuel 10/2008, Elle 03/2008 / Condé Nast, Barrierefreies Wohnen, architektur . BAYERN 2008 / Otto - exxtra-Werbung, Barzón (Buenos Aires, Argentina) April 2008, edition:schwaben - architektur bauen garten & wohnen / edition schwaben, Häuser Special, Die 100 Besten Einfamilienhaus-Architekten, Das Neubau-Buch, Purissimo/ Aktuelle Beispiele minimalistischer Wohnhäuser, Individuelle Küchen/ Maßgeschneidert von Architekten, Designern und Schreinern, AIT 03/2008, 50 Wohlfühl-Häuser, A&W Special, 2. Wessobrunner Architekturpreis 2008

998335
ANNIKA
Lotte Mi
45 €
0173 9498521
Bogenhausen
Herzogpark
Thomas Spies
01729590550
150/200 €

ELVITAL

2004
OCT
6
WED AM
LOLITA PILLE

8a

TERENCE CONRAN
SEIDE

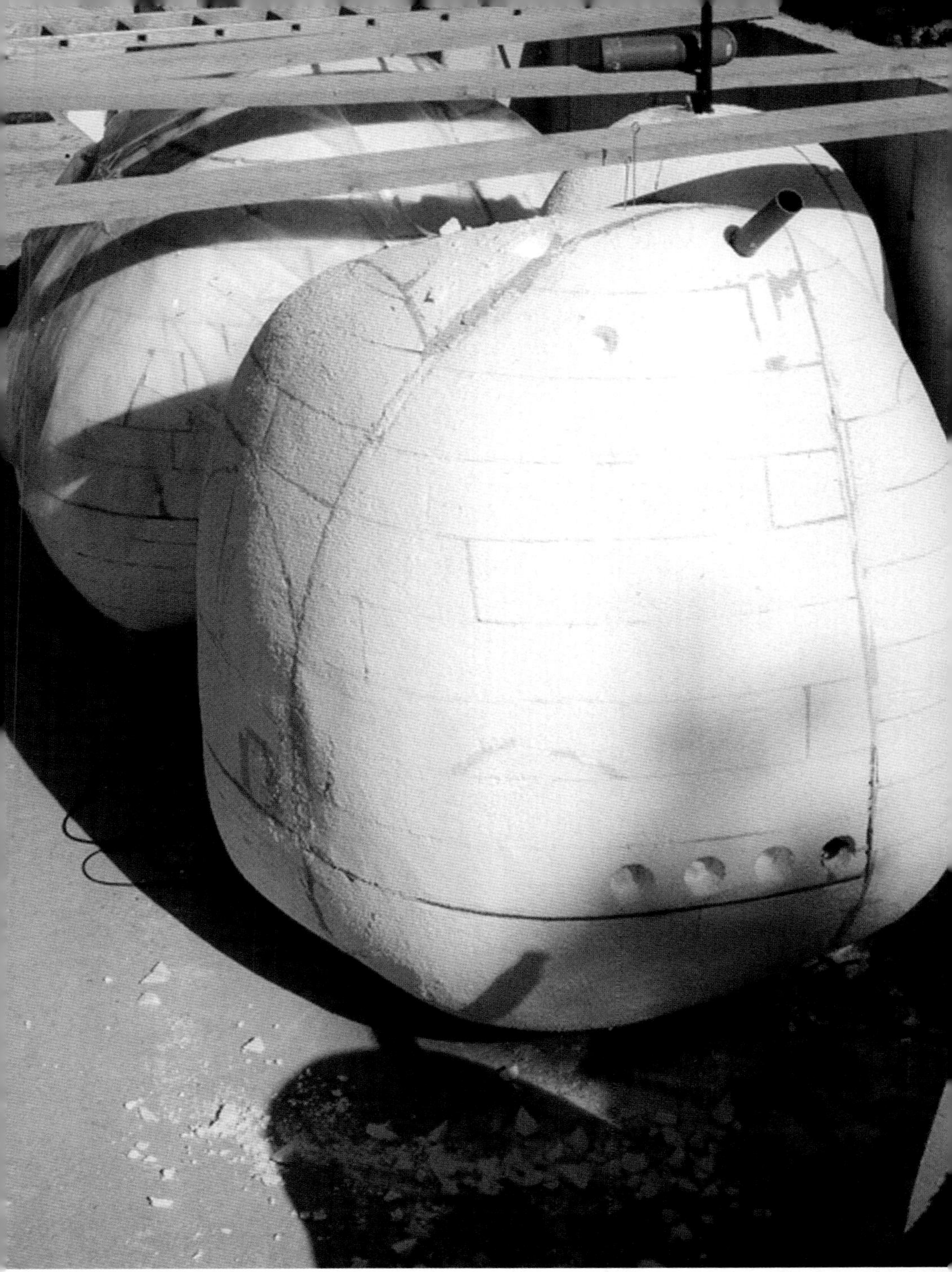

003 ATELIER IM CURRYPARK Studio in Currypark

>677

 003 ATELIER IM CURRYPARK Studio in Currypark

7

LIEB

403 DIÖZESANKURIE ROTTENBURG Rottenburg Bishop's Diocese

>680

007 HAUS MIT PRAXIS Single-family home with surgery

>681

405 NRW- BANK IN MÜNSTER Münster NRW - Bank

>682

2005

>683

406 ERWEITERUNG DER STADTHALLE Town hall extension

>684

406 ERWEITERUNG DER STADTHALLE Town hall extension

>684

013 WOHNBEBAUUNG LACHEN-BIRKENALLEE Lachen-Birkenallee residential area

>685

2007

 014 HOLZSTOSS Stack of logs >686

2001

GROSSER PREIS
FÜR ALPINE
ARCHITEKTUR
www.wessobrunner-kreis.de

ROSSER PREIS
FÜR ALPINE
RCHITEKTUR

 015 WOHNANLAGE GARTENSRTASSE Gartenstrasse residential complex >687

2006

>688

2000

>689

2000

 407 WOHNBEBAUUNG SEDANSTRASSE Sedanstrasse esidential area >690

024 WOHNBEBAUUNG PÖCKING Pöcking residential complex

>691

024 WOHNBEBAUUNG PÖCKING Pöcking residential complex

>691

>693

 409 EUROPÄISCHE SCHULE European school

2007

029 ZWILLINGSHAUS GRAFRATH Grafrath twin house

>694

 029 ZWILLINGSHAUS GRAFRATH Grafrath twin house >694

410 JUGENDHAUS DER VERSTÄNDIGUNG Youth centre for communication

>695

410 **JUGENDHAUS DER VERSTÄNDIGUNG** Youth centre for communication

>695

030 ALTER SPORTPLATZ IN SCHONDORF Schondorf former sports ground

>696

030 ALTER SPORTPLATZ IN SCHONDORF Schondorf former sports ground

>656

030 ALTER SPORTPLATZ IN SCHONDORF Schondorf former sports ground

>696

BIZE
L'ARLES

BIZET:
ARLESIENNE

2005

KATSU
KUNST

037.1 FREMDENVERKEHRSAMT LANDSBERG AM LECH Landsberg am Lech tourist office

>702

037.1 FREMDENVERKEHRSAMT LANDSBERG AM LECH Landsberg am Lech tourist office

>702

037.1 FREMDENVERKEHRSAMT LANDSBERG AM LECH Landsberg am Lech tourist office

>702

 037.1 FREMDENVERKEHRSAMT LANDSBERG AM LECH Landsberg am Lech tourist office >702

037.2 RATHAUS LANDSBERG AM LECH Landsberg am Lech city council

>703

037.2 RATHAUS LANDSBERG AM LECH Landsberg am Lech city council

>703

037.2 RATHAUS LANDSBERG AM LECH Landsberg am Lech city council

>703

 037.2 RATHAUS LANDSBERG AM LECH Landsberg am Lech city council >703

037.2 RATHAUS LANDSBERG AM LECH Landsberg am Lech city council

>703

 037.2 RATHAUS LANDSBERG AM LECH Landsberg am Lech city council >703

2009

037.2 RATHAUS LANDSBERG AM LECH Landsberg am Lech city council

>703

037.2 RATHAUS LANDSBERG AM LECH Landsberg am Lech city council

>703

037.2 RATHAUS LANDSBERG AM LECH Landsberg am Lech city council

>703

>704

Reinhard Sig

Irminfriedstraße
Geiger

 415 STADTMUSEUM KAUFBEUREN Kaufbeuren town museum >706

>708

21.

> 709

044 SPARKASSE MIT REIHENHÄUSERN Sparkasse branch office with terraced houses

>710

044 SPARKASSE MIT REIHENHÄUSERN Sparkasse branch office with terraced houses

>710

044 SPARKASSE MIT REIHENHÄUSERN Sparkasse branch office with terraced houses

>710

2

044 SPARKASSE MIT REIHENHÄUSERN Sparkasse branch office with terraced houses

>710

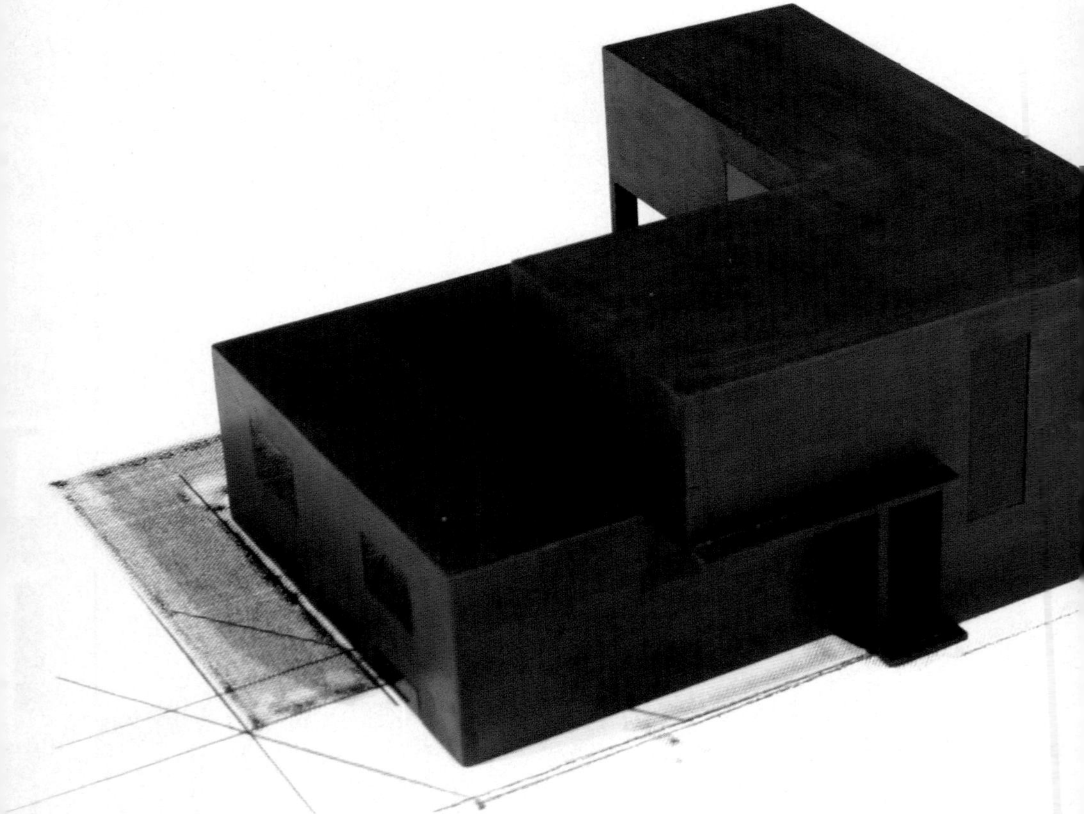

418 SEEANLAGEN DIESSEN Diessen lake complex

>714

418 SEEANLAGEN DIESSEN Diessen lake complex

>714

Michael Weber

URBAN
WEBER
BAU GMBH

 >718

7

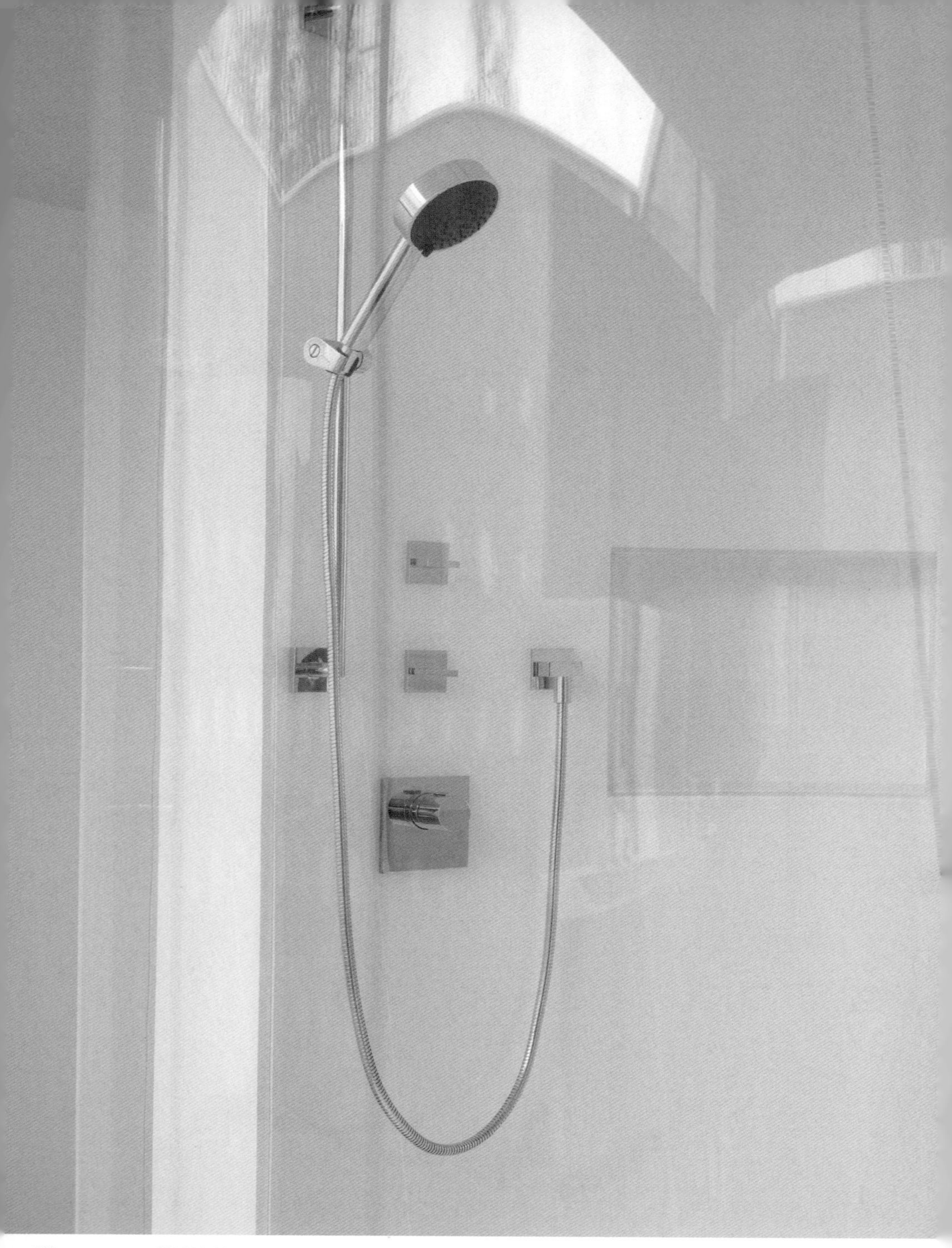

>718

420 BÜRGER - UND KULTURZENTRUM ALTÖTTING Altötting cultural and community centre

>719

420 BÜRGER - UND KULTURZENTRUM ALTÖTTING Altötting cultural and community centre

>719

421 JUGENDHAUS NEUGABLONZ Neugablonz youth centre

>722

421 JUGENDHAUS NEUGABLONZ Neugablonz youth centre

>722

 423 STÄDTEBAU „AUBING - OST“ Urban planning „Aubing - Ost“ >724

423 STÄDTEBAU „AUBING - OST“ Urban planning „Aubing - Ost“

>724

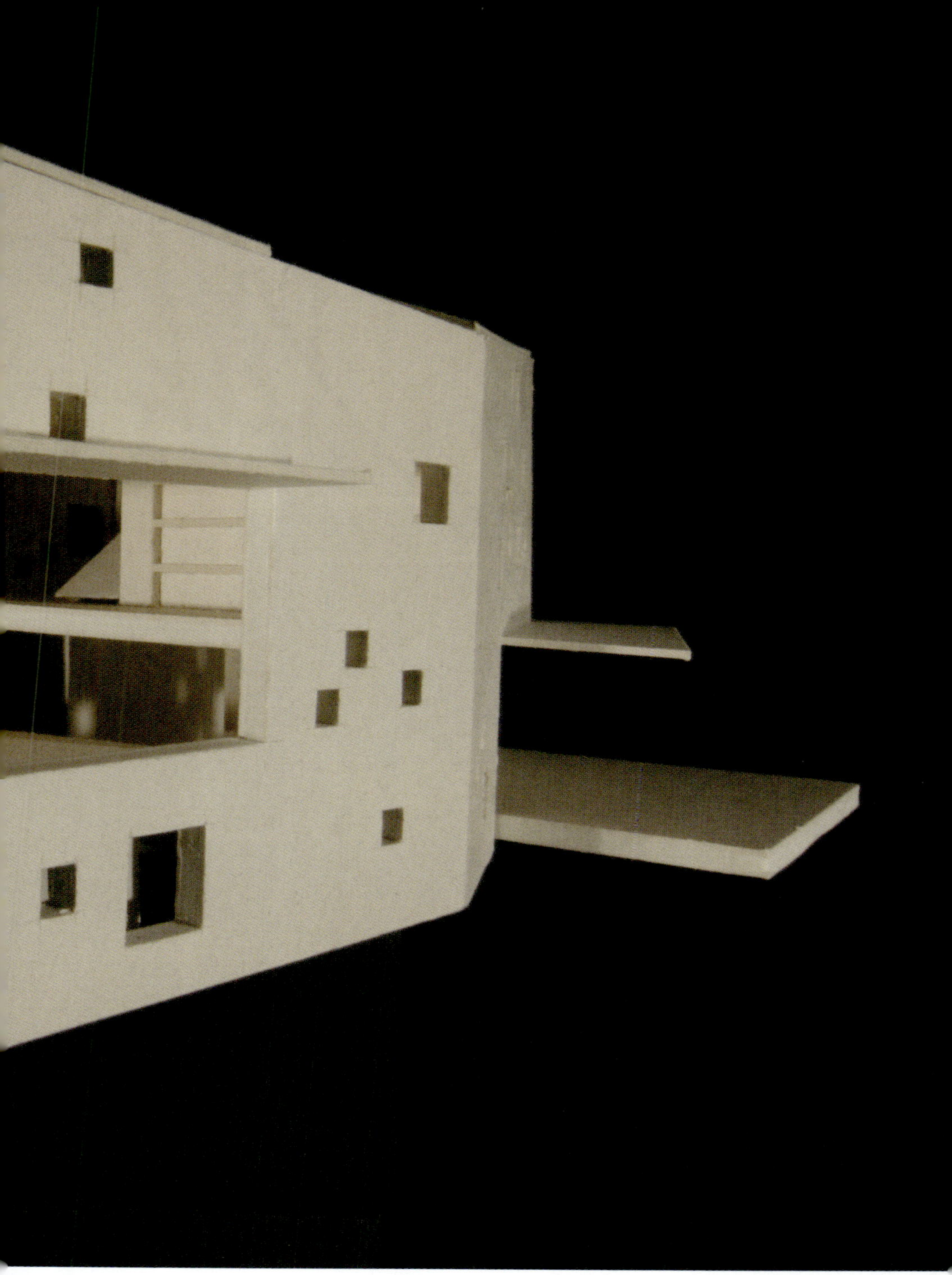

2009

Material-Container 3-to. Gesamtlast

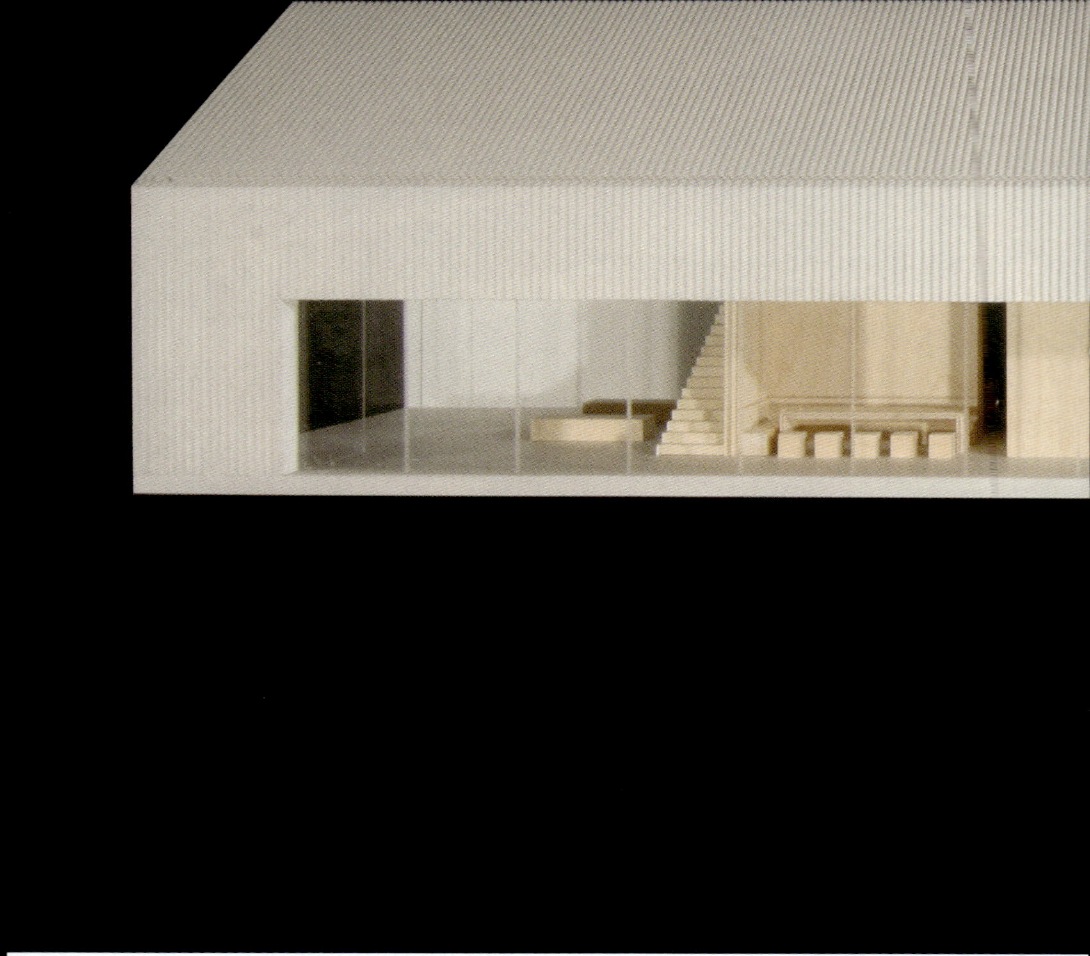

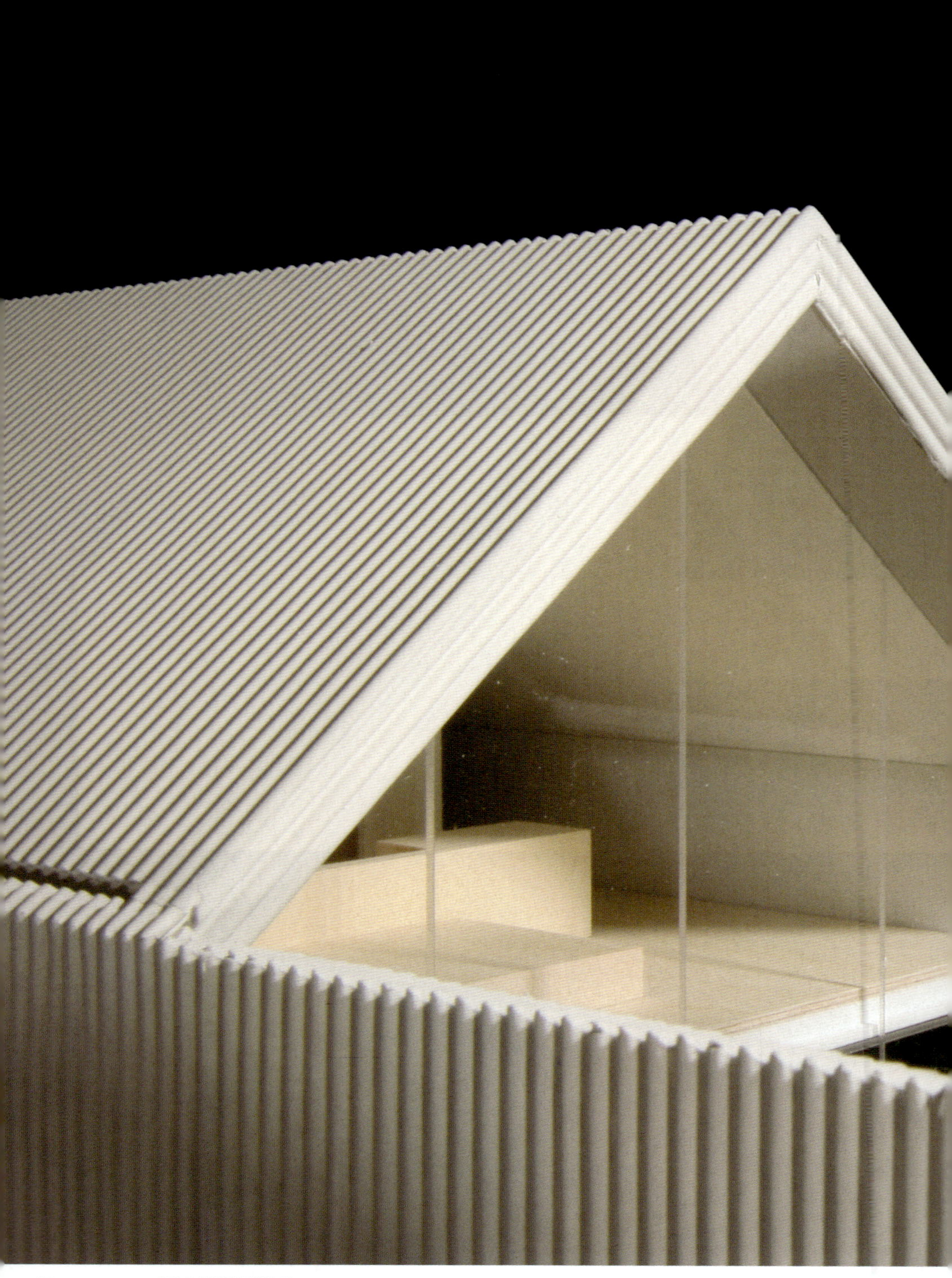

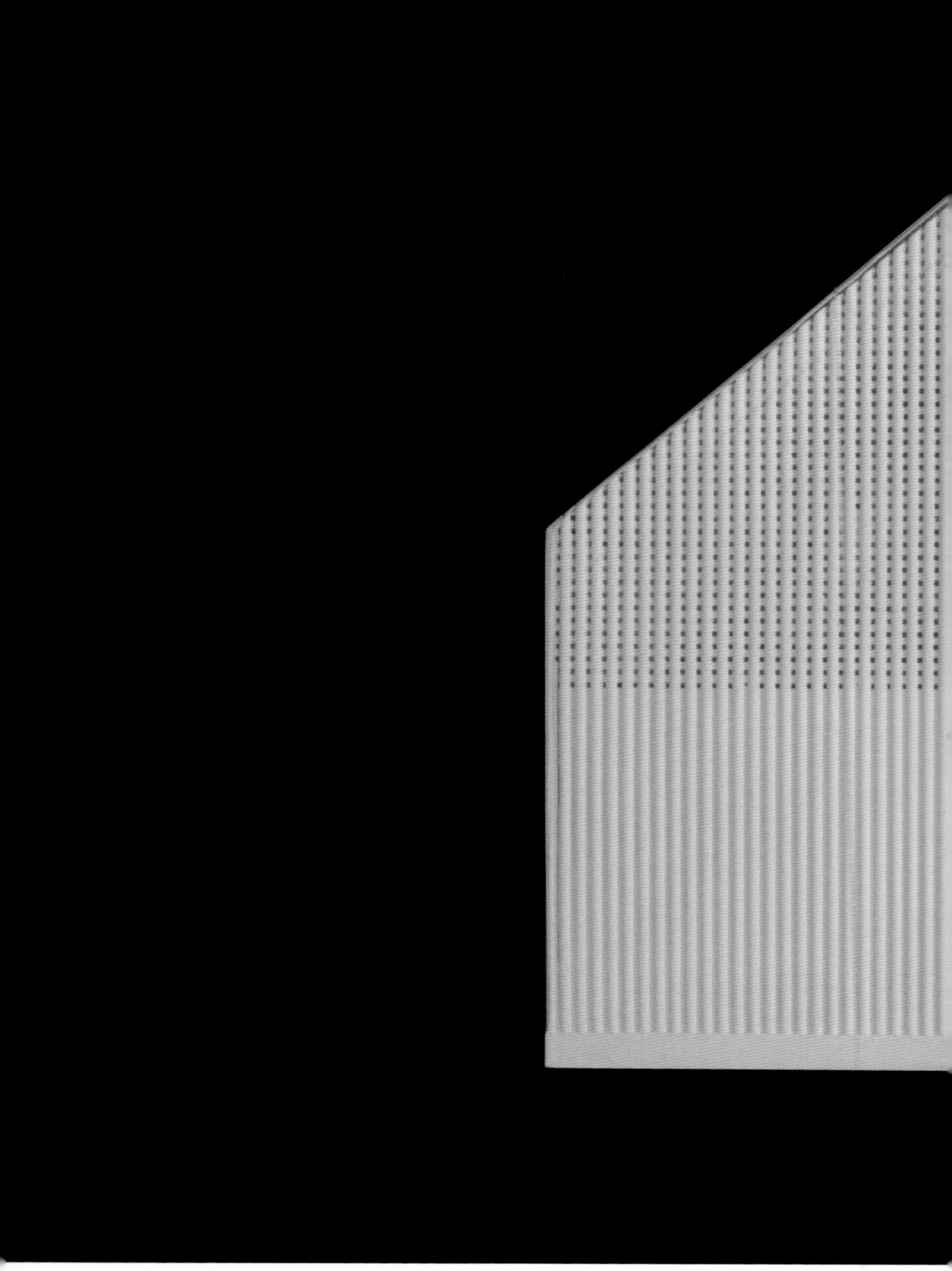

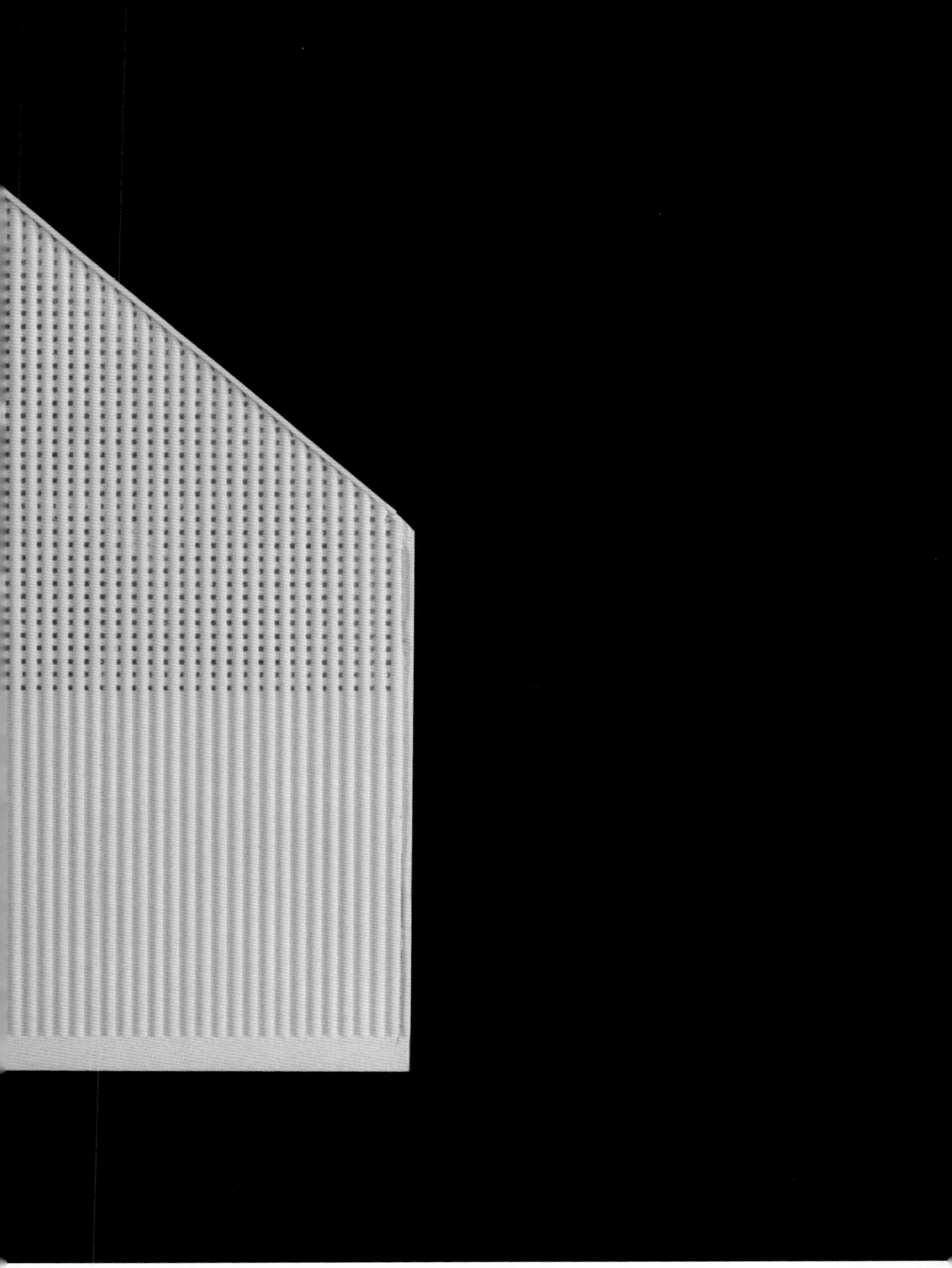

5
BÜ

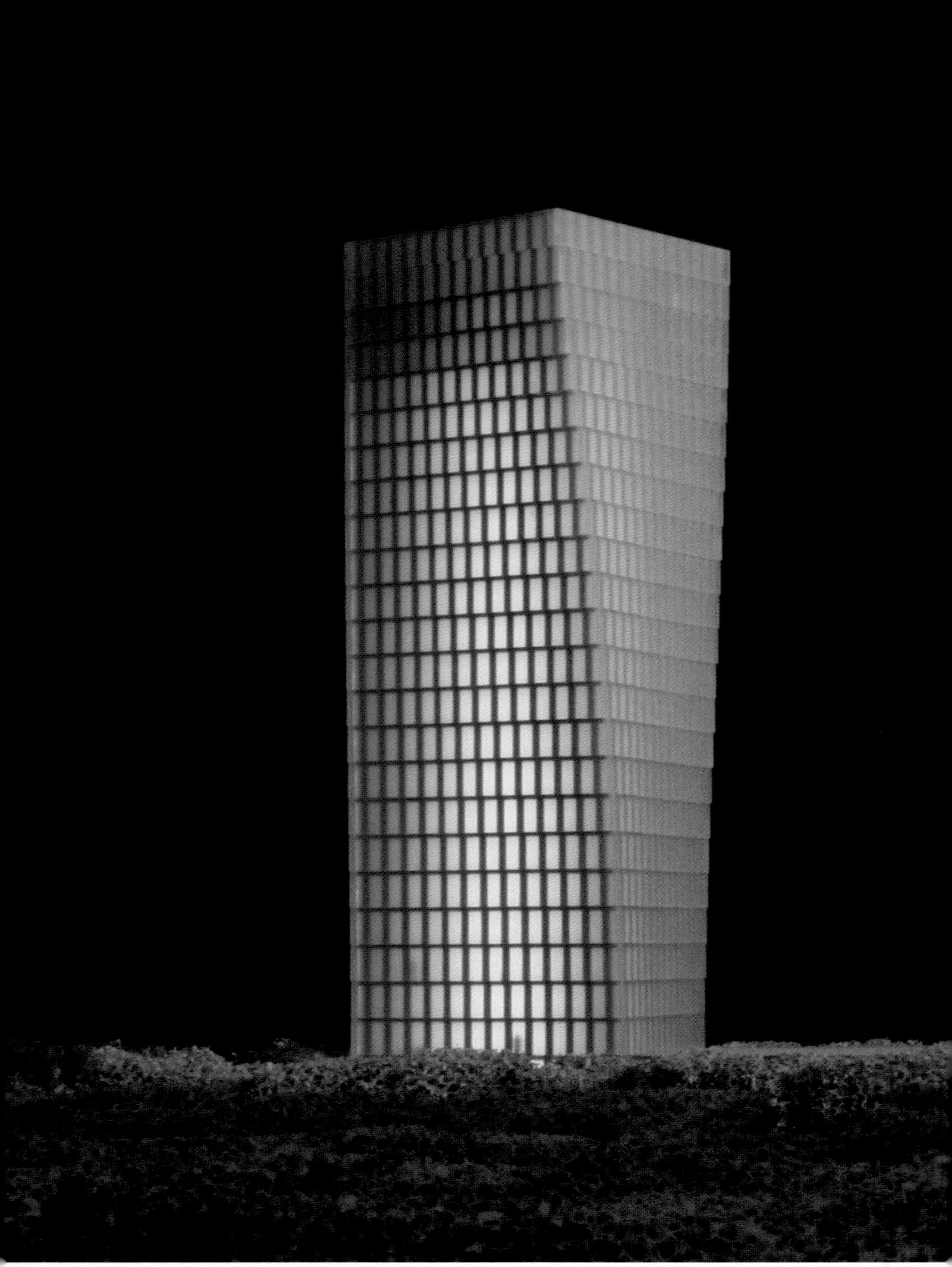

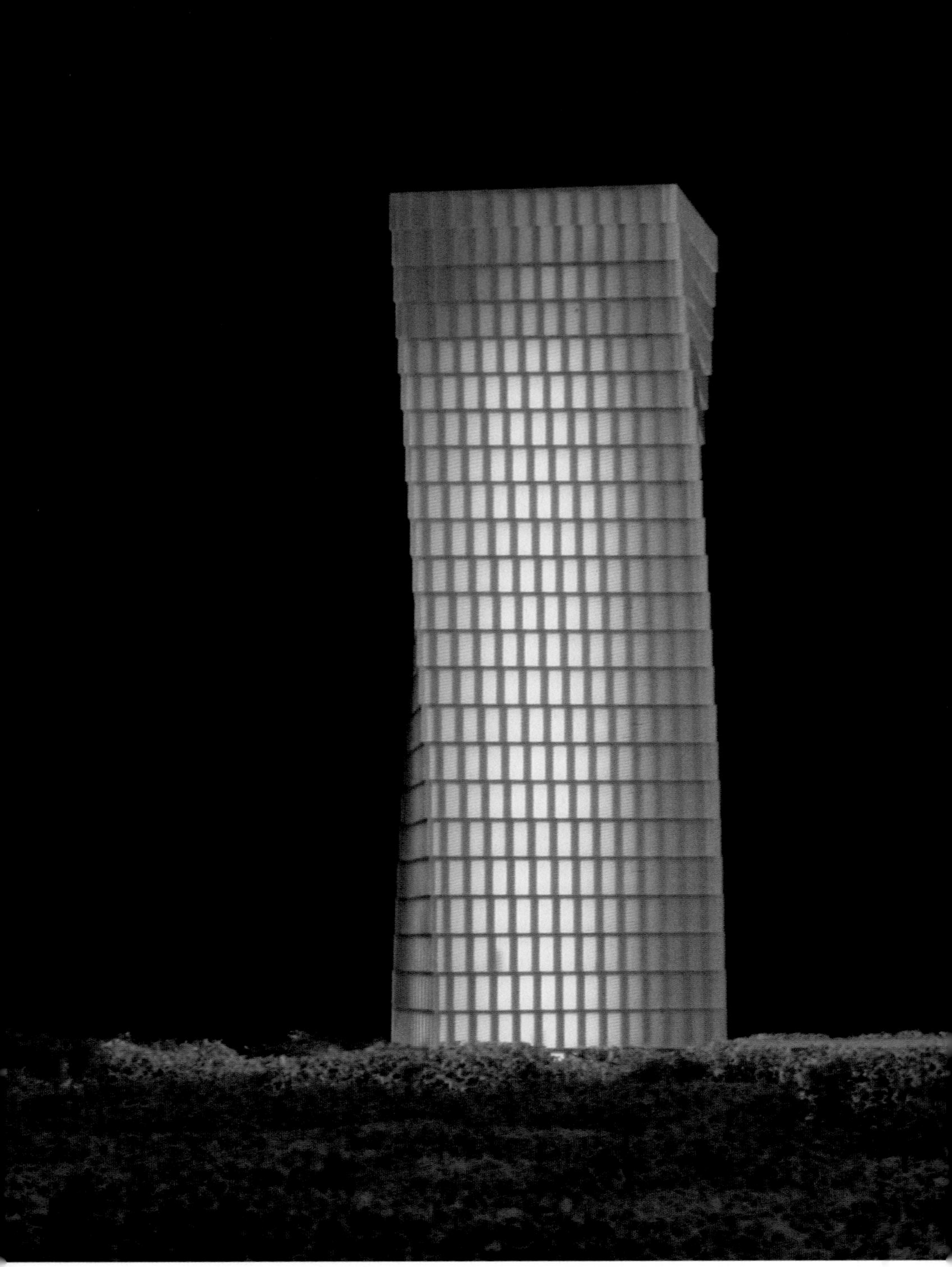

430 HOTELANLAGE NÜRNBERG Nuremberg hotel complex

>731

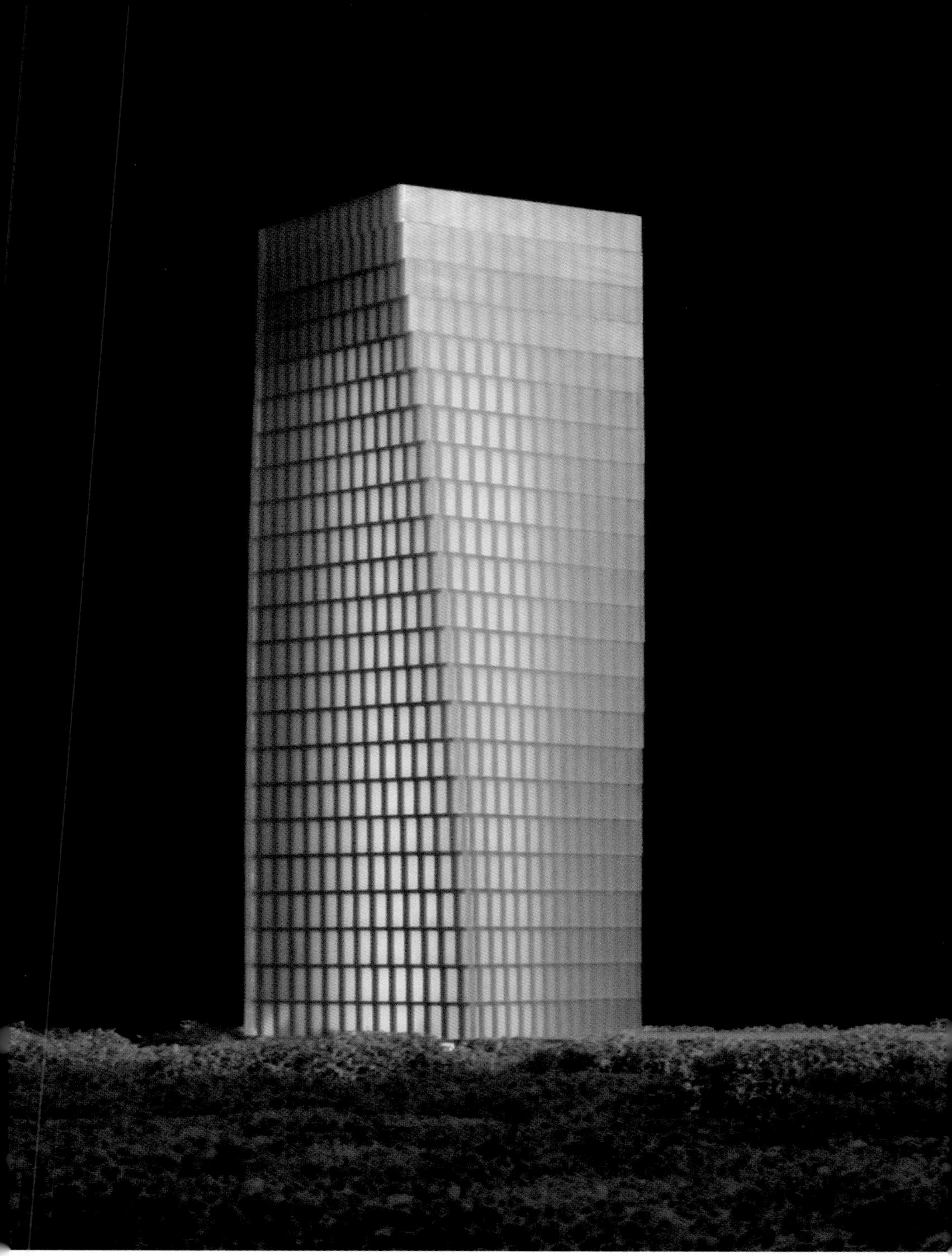

>732

1 2 3 4

087 GRUNDSCHULE HOLZKIRCHEN Holzkirchen primary school

>733

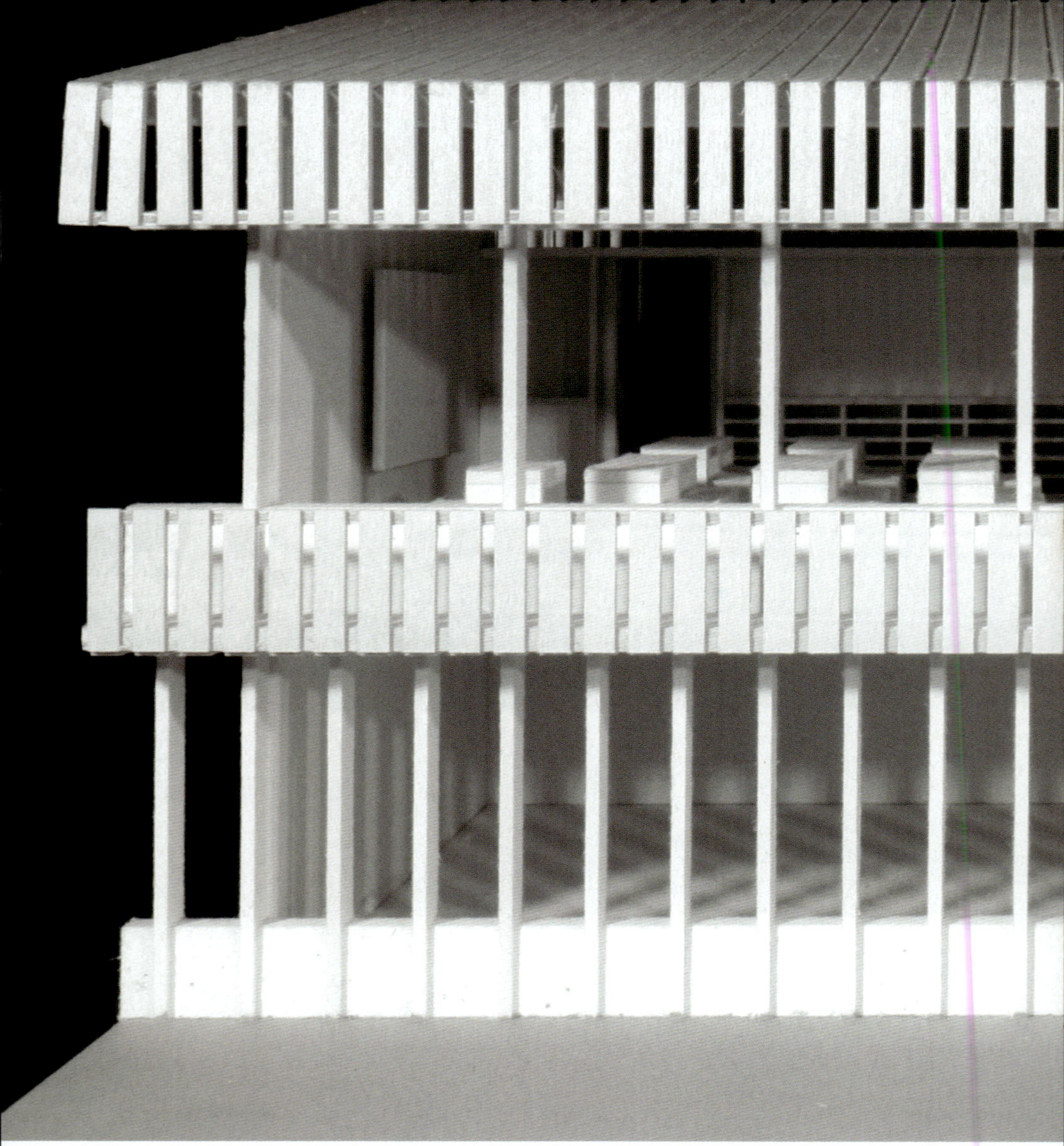

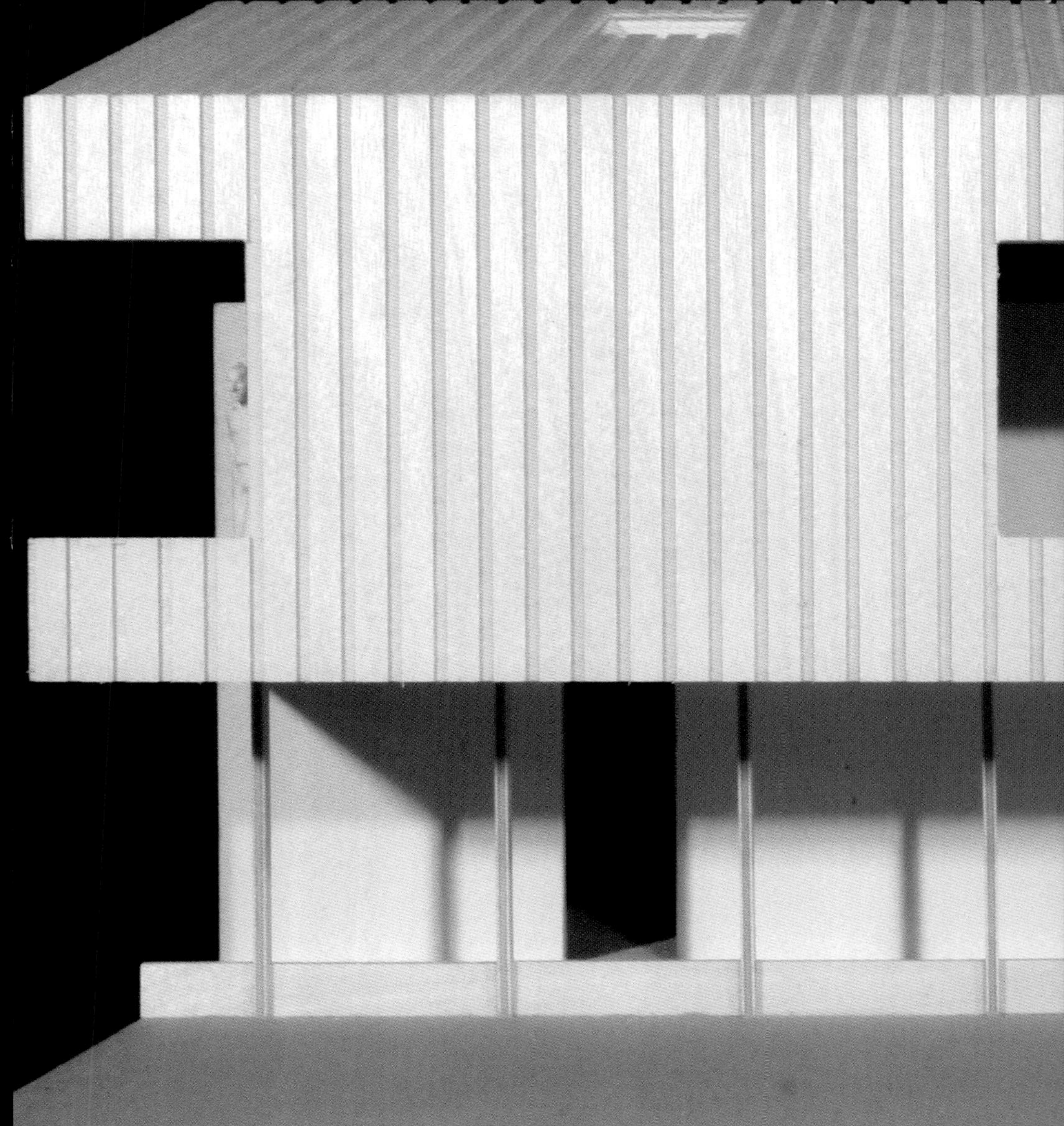

433 RATHAUS WETTSTETTEN Wettstetten town hall

>735

 433 RATHAUS WETTSTETTEN Wettstetten town hall ≥735

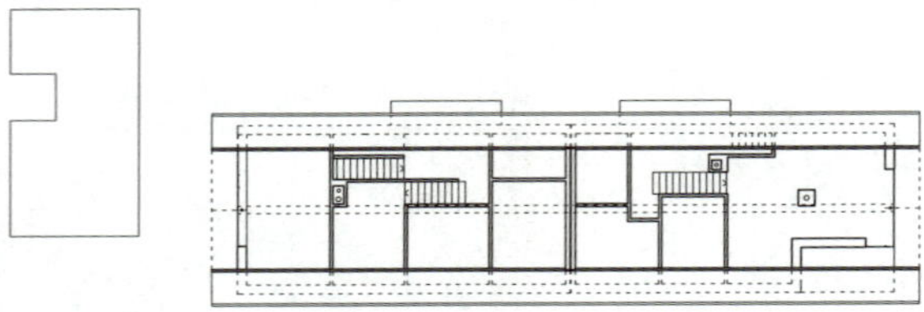

DG

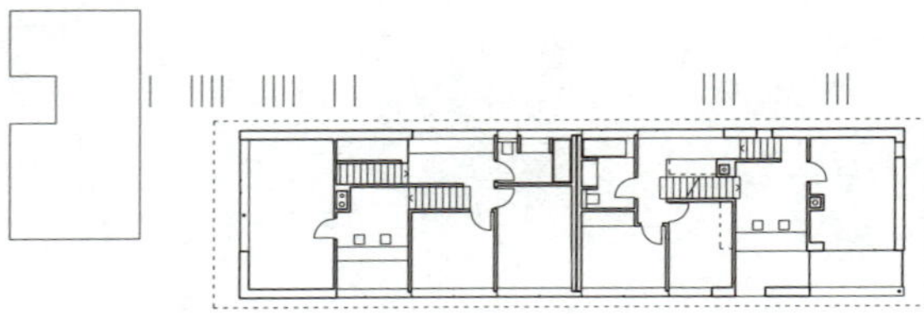

OG

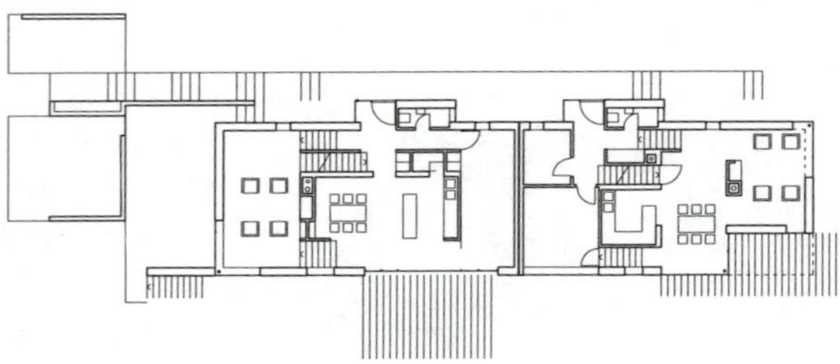

EG

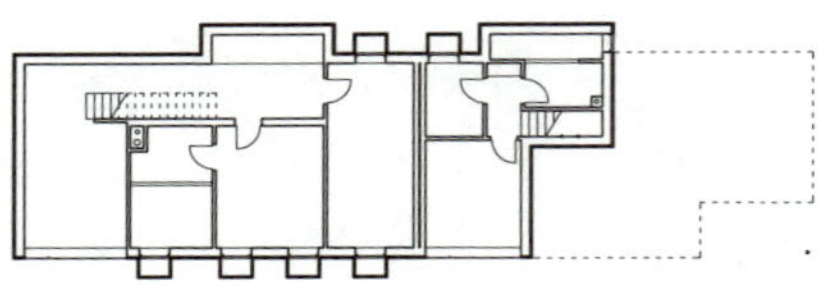

UG

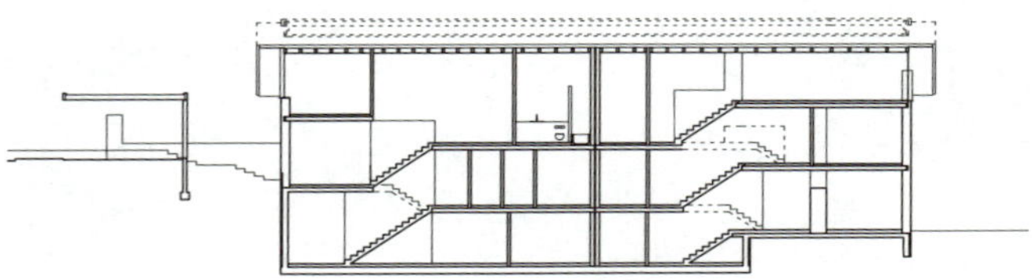

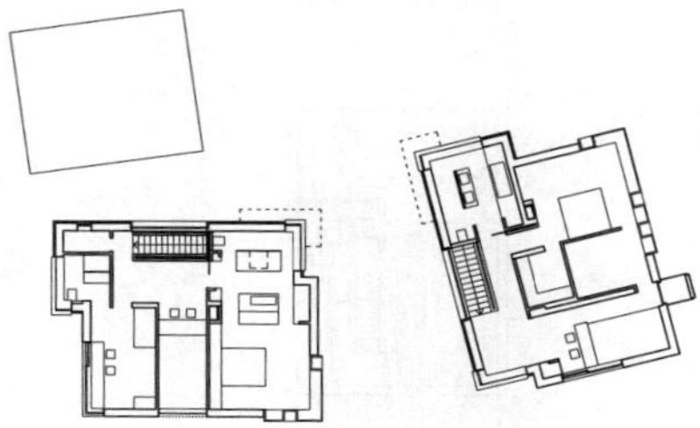

OG

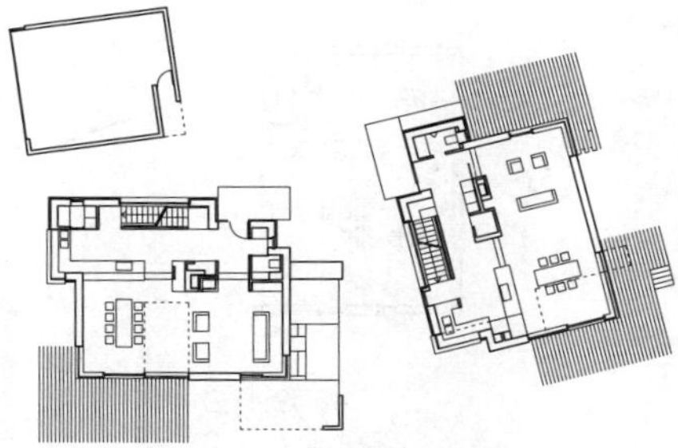

EG

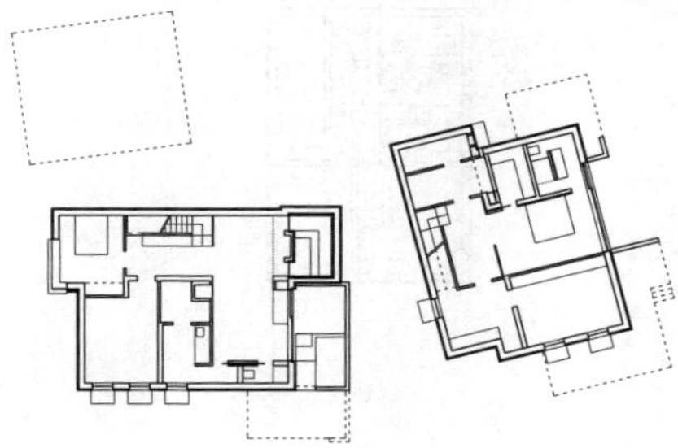

UG

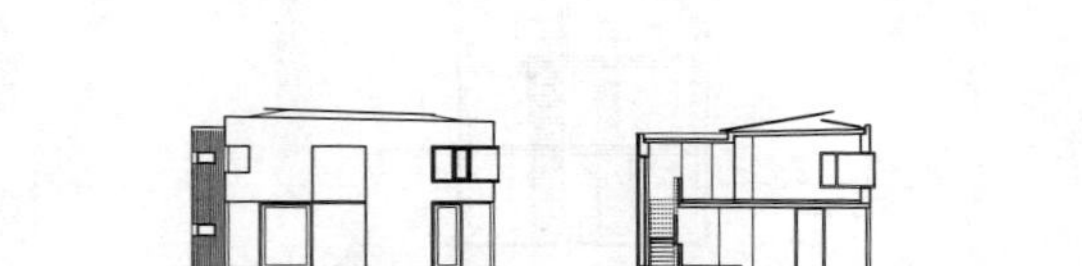

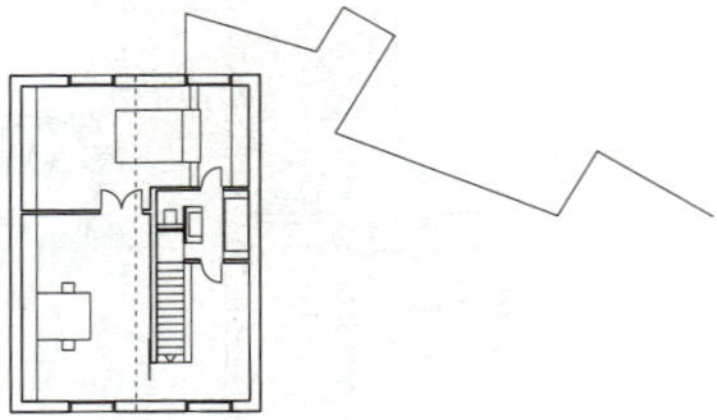

DG

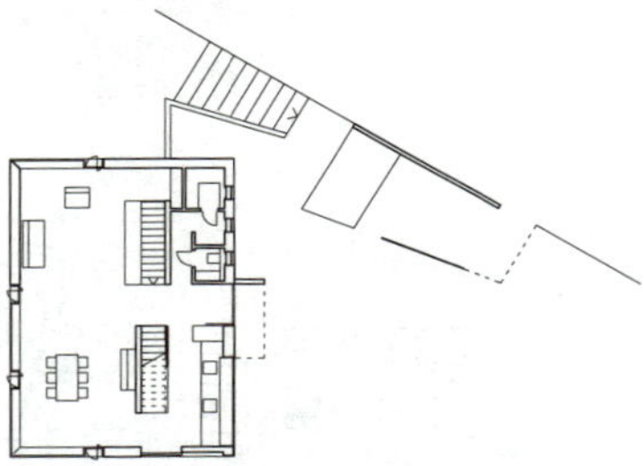

OG

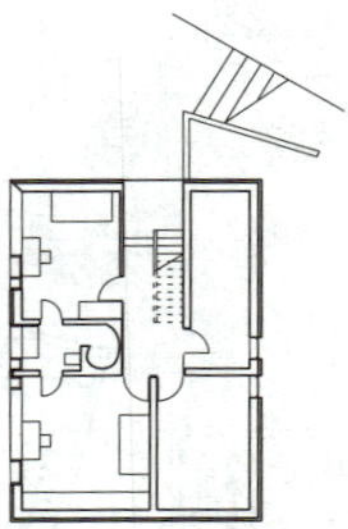

EG

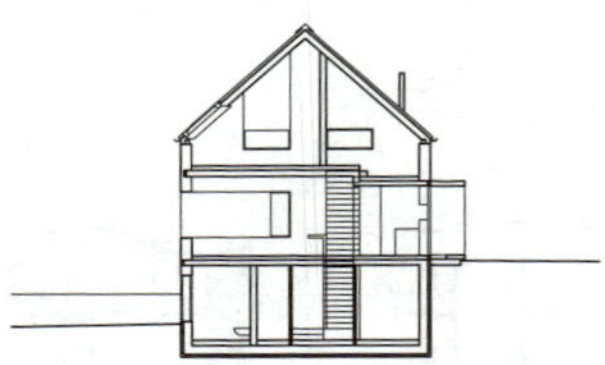

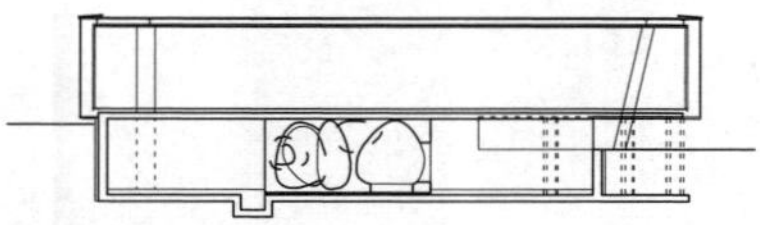

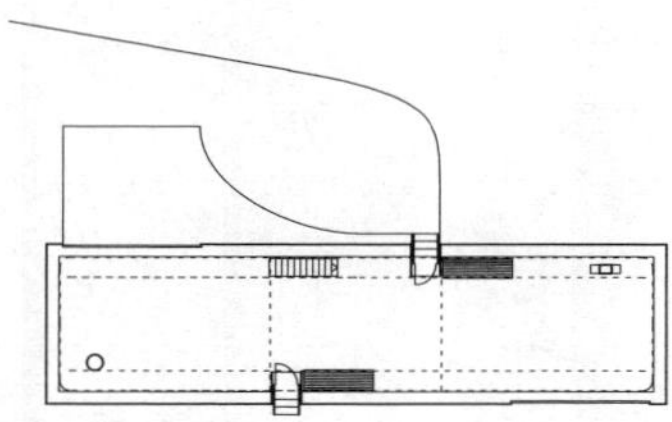

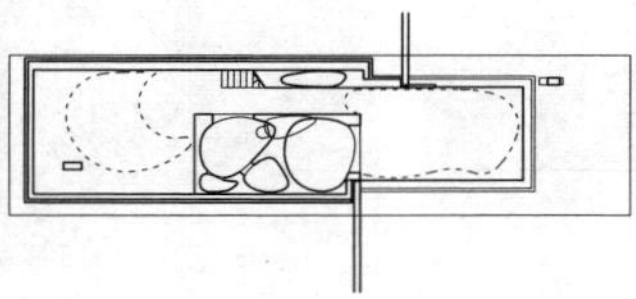

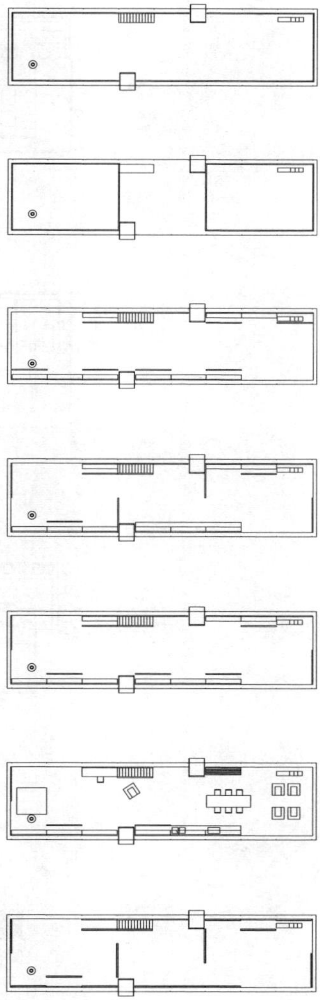

OG

EG

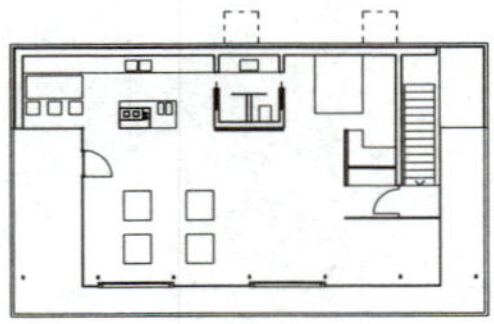

DG

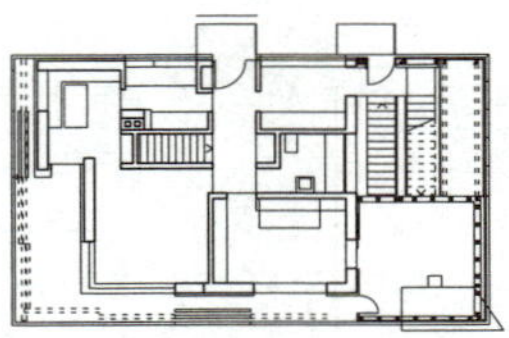

OG

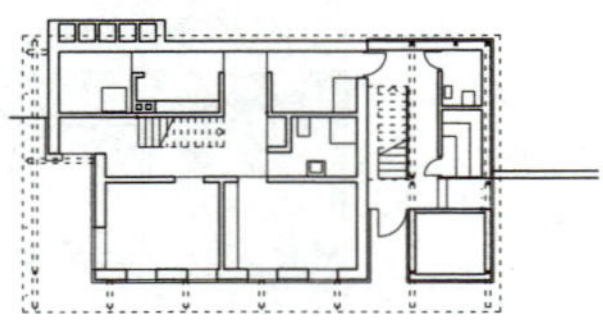

EG

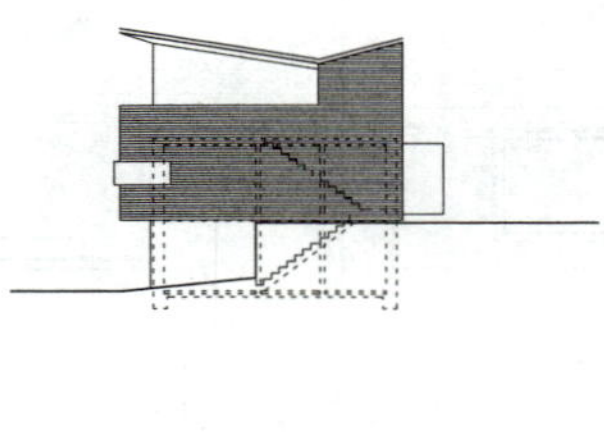

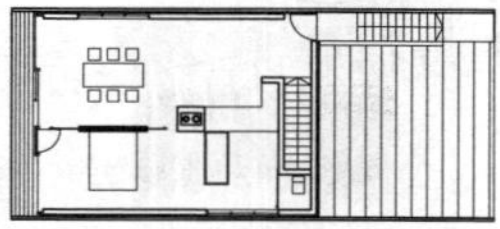

OG

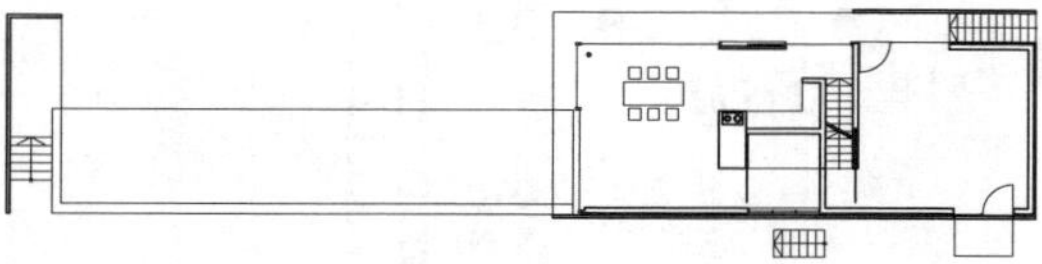

EG

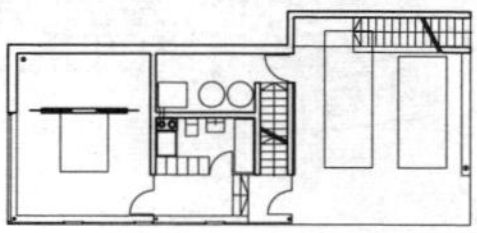

UG

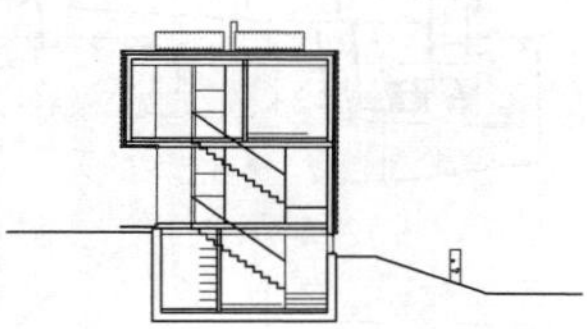

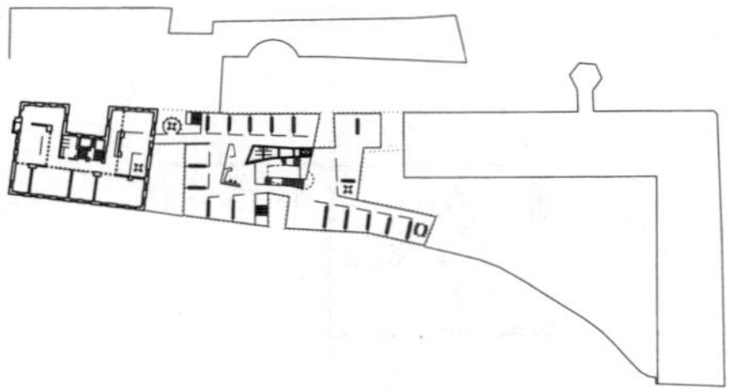

2.OG

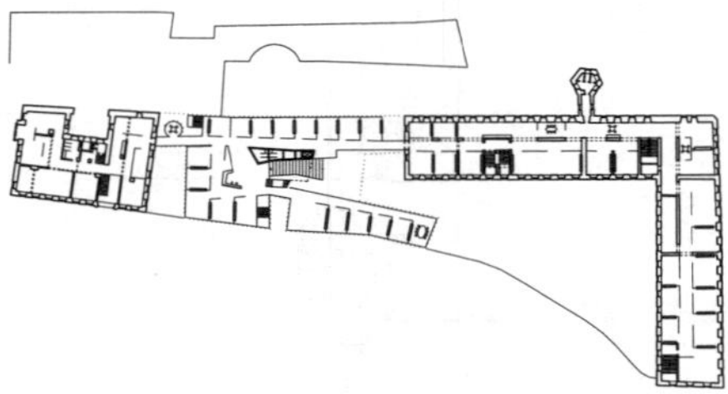

1.OG

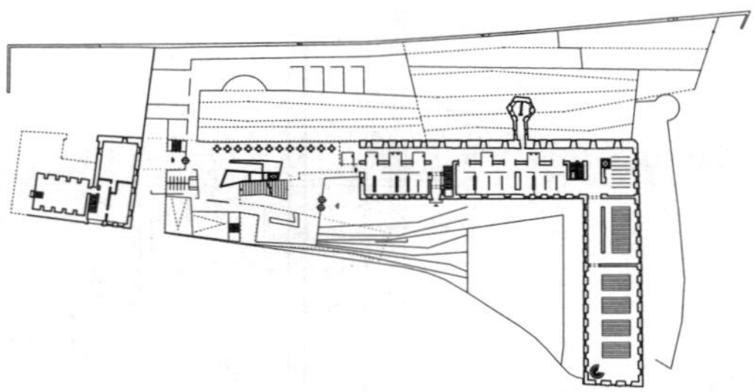

EG

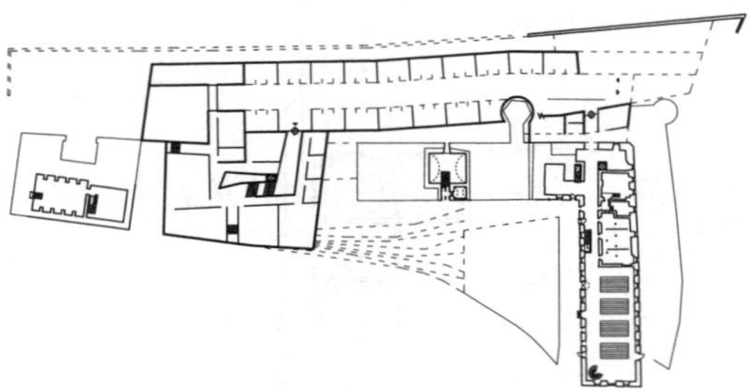

UG

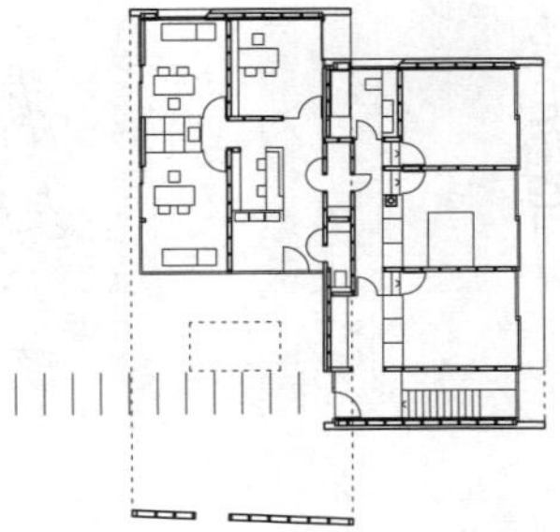

OG

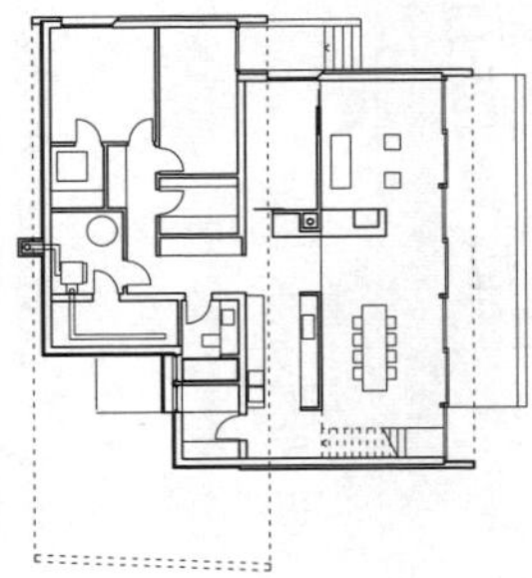

EG

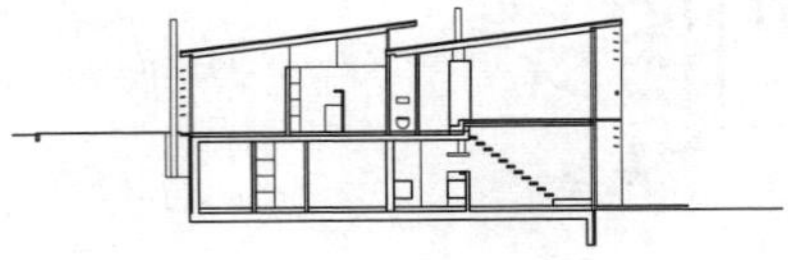

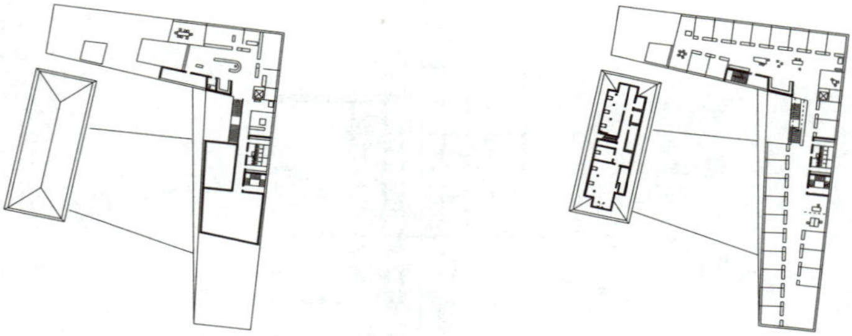

5.OG | 4.OG

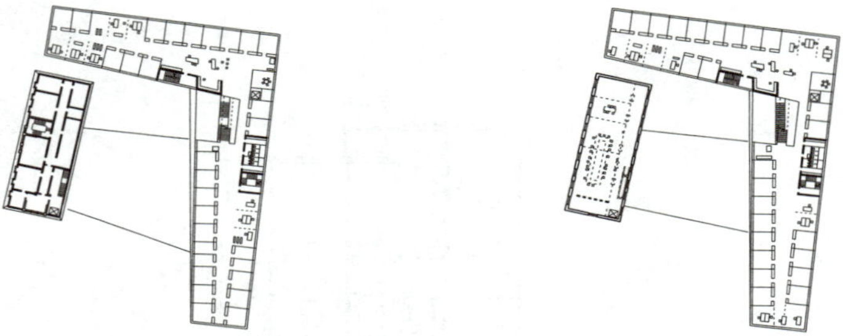

3.OG | 2.OG

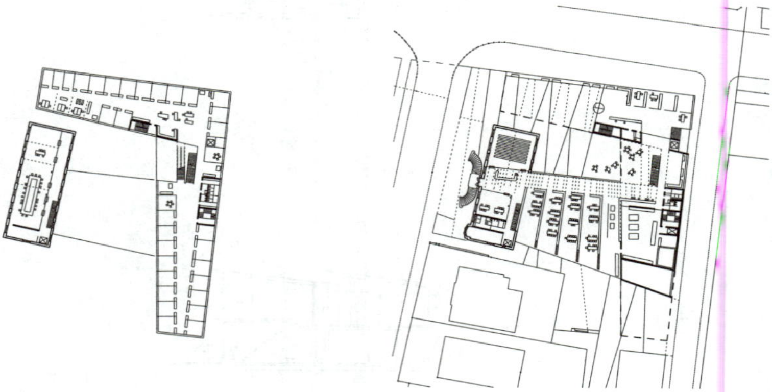

1.OG | EG

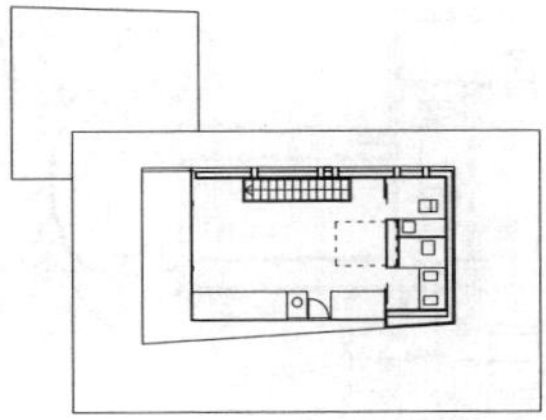

DG

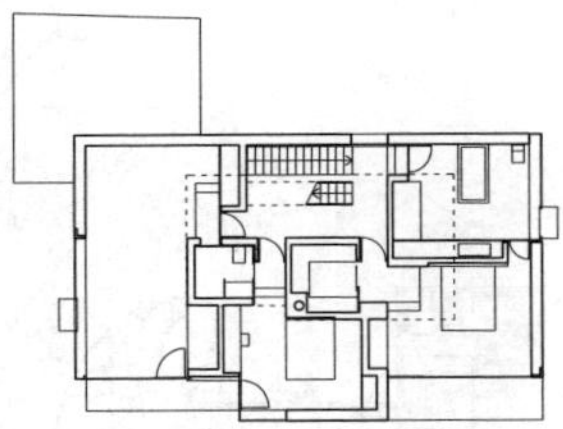

OG

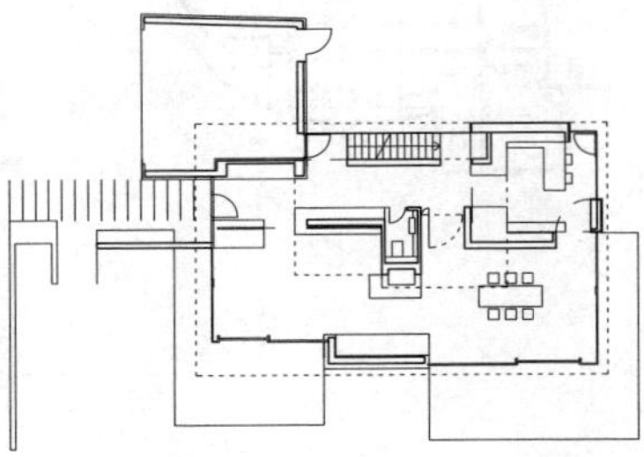

EG

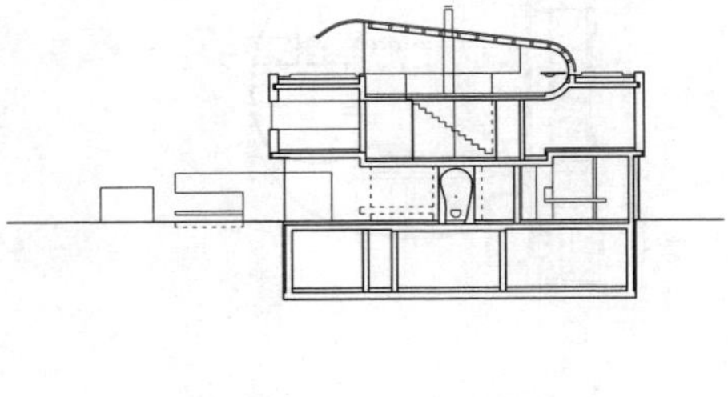

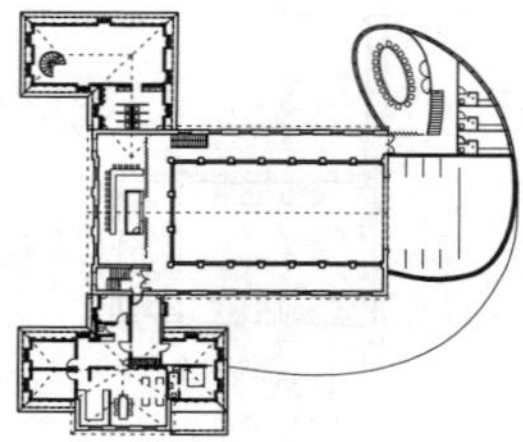

DG

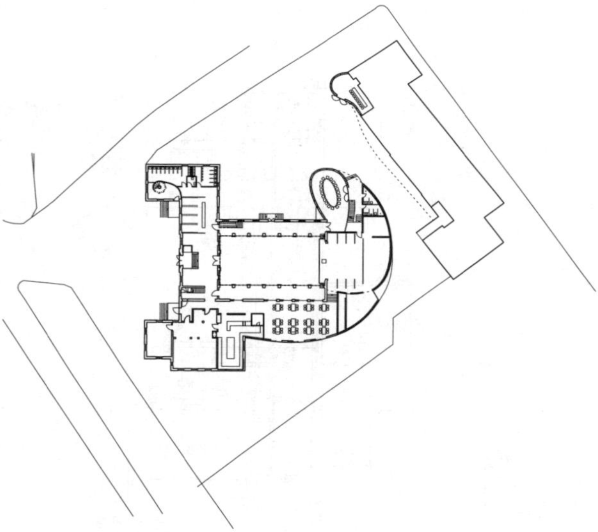

EG

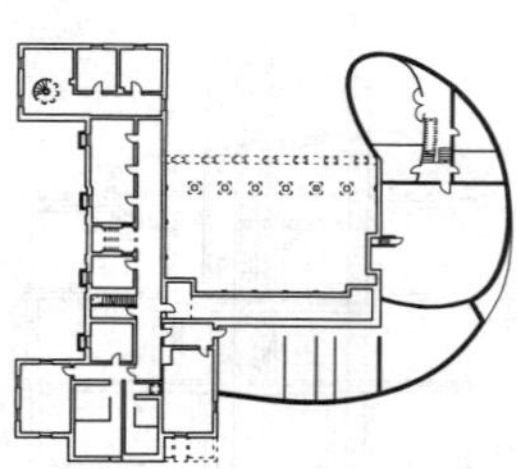

UG

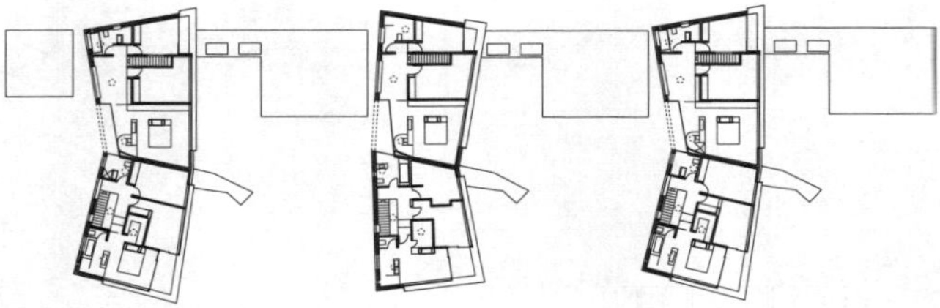

OG

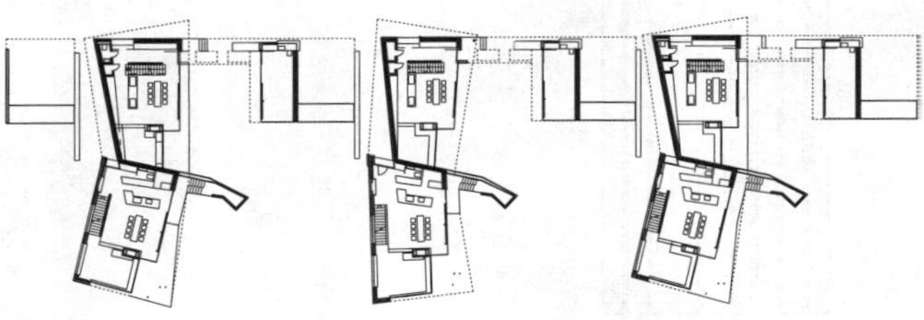

EG

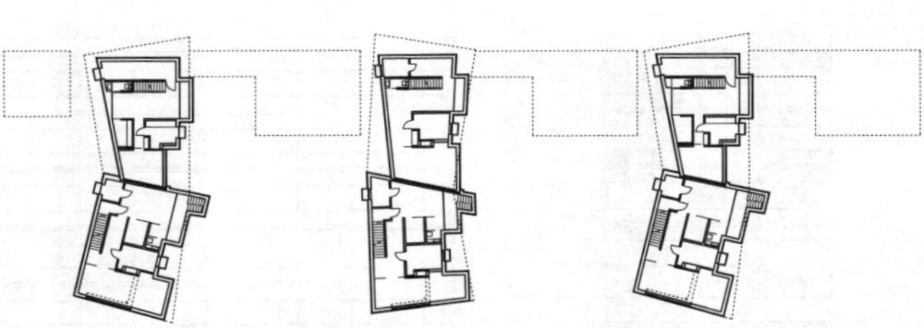

UG

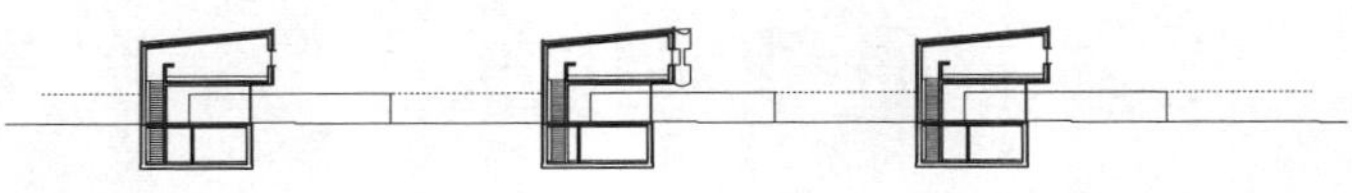

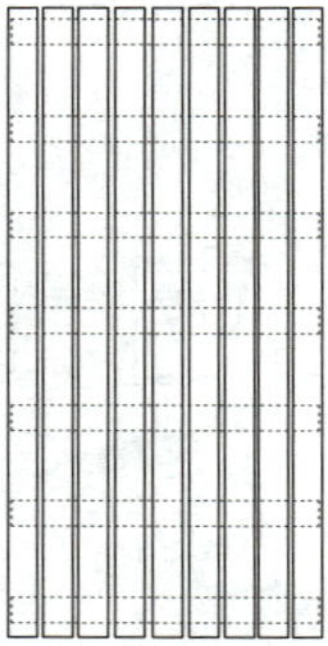

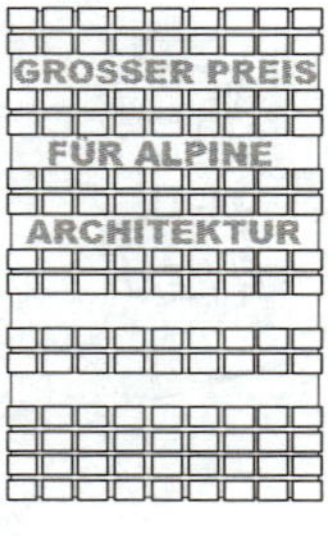
GROSSER PREIS
FÜR ALPINE
ARCHITEKTUR

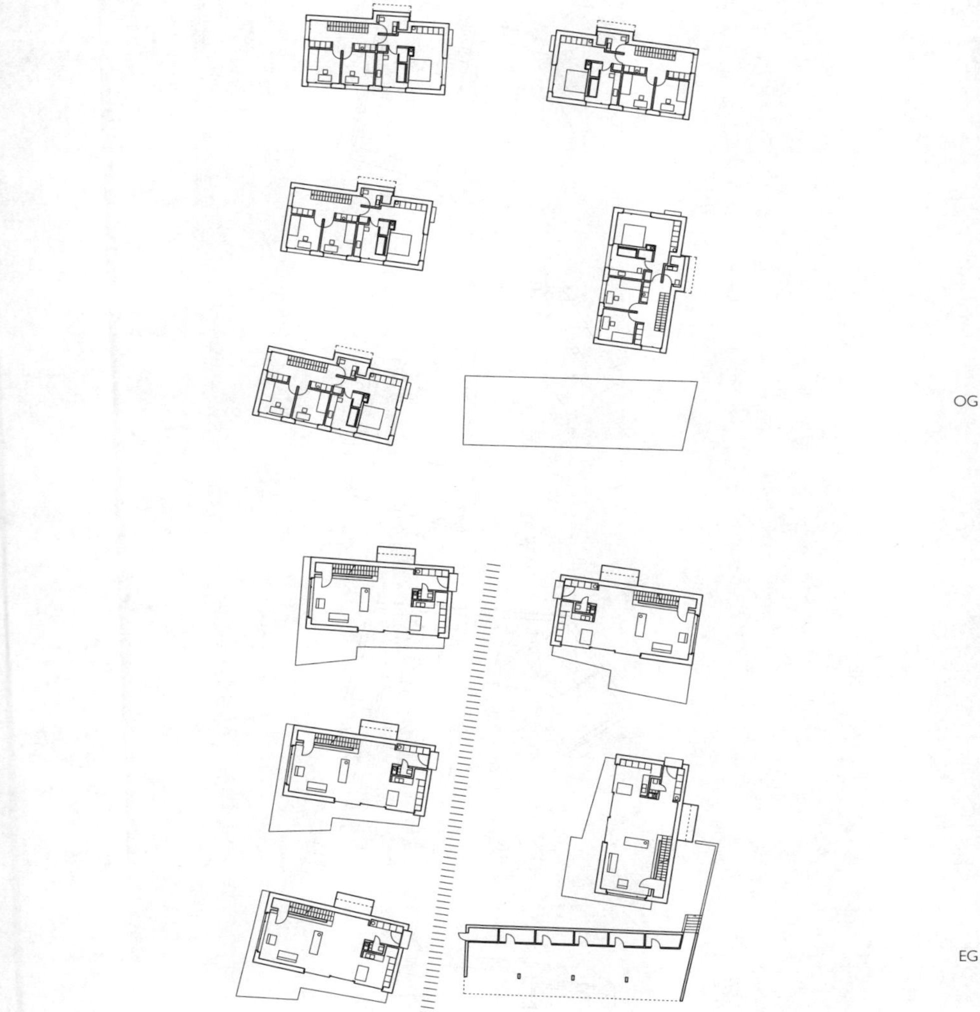
OG
EG

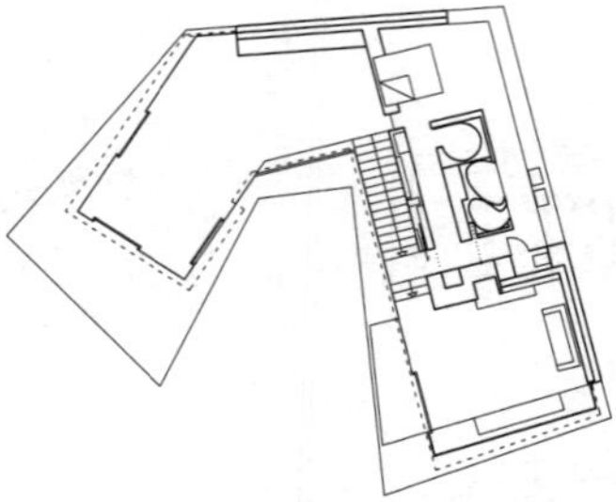

OG

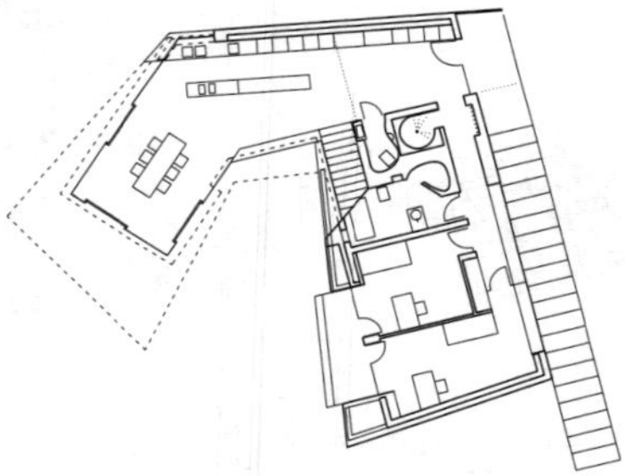

EG

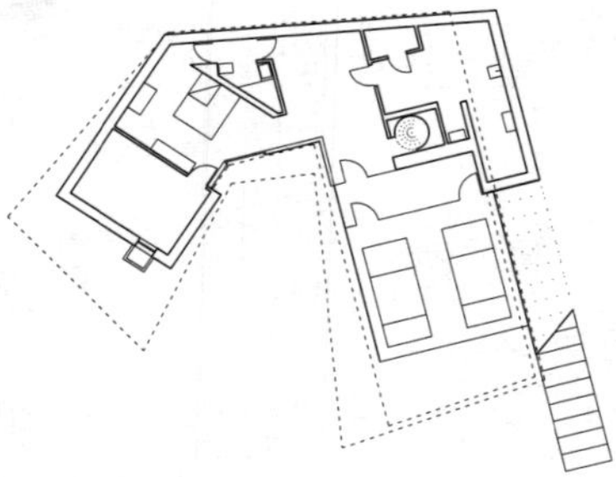

UG

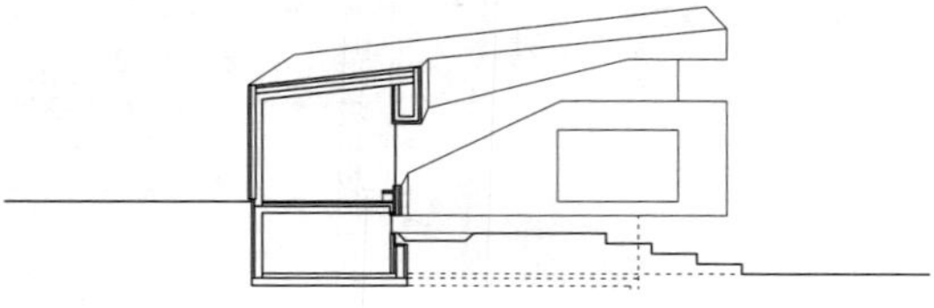

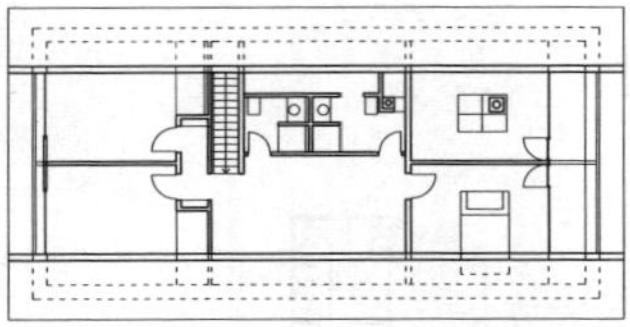

DG

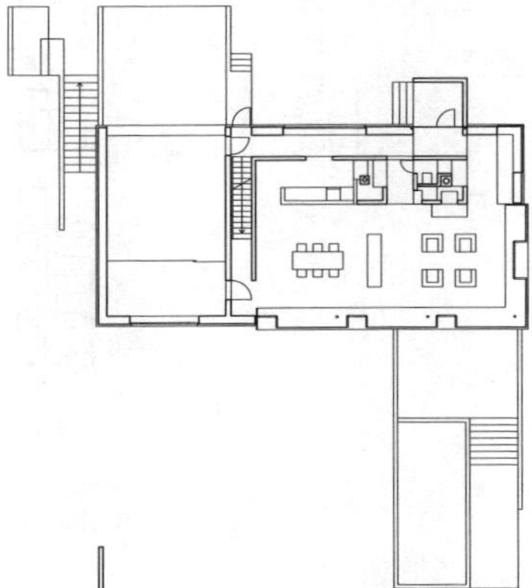

OG

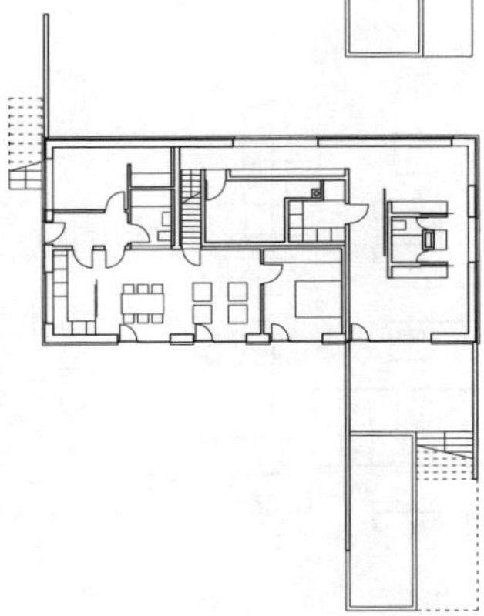

EG

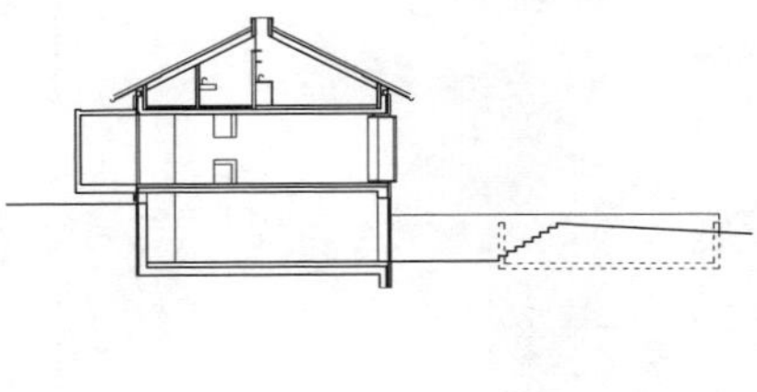

2.OG | 1.OG

EG | UG

OG

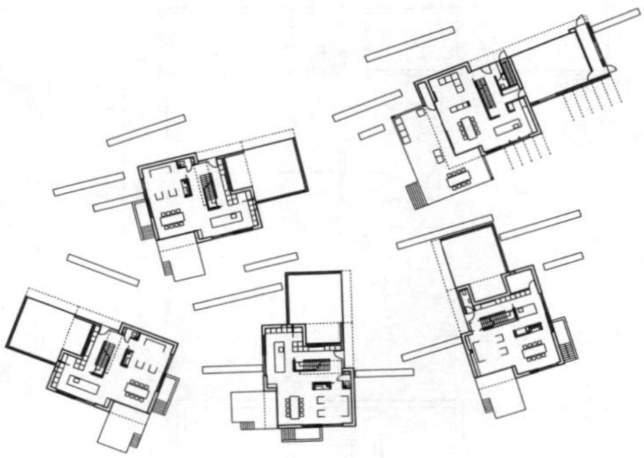

EG

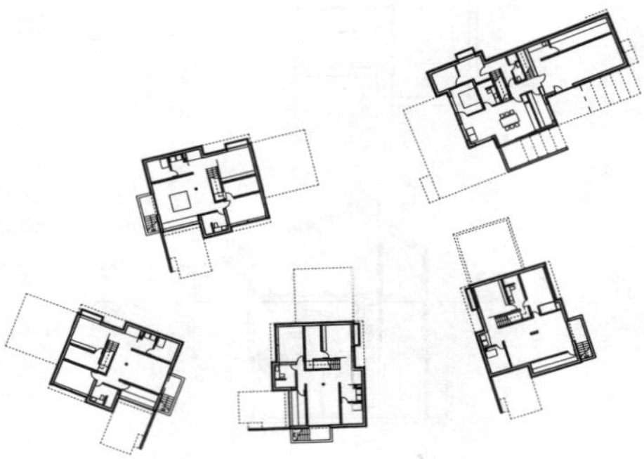

UG

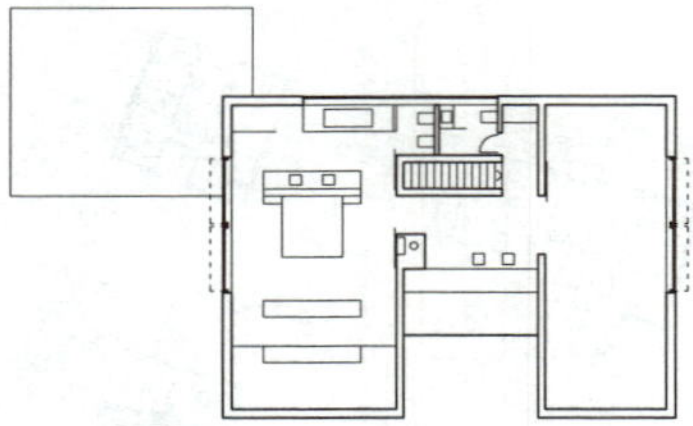

DG

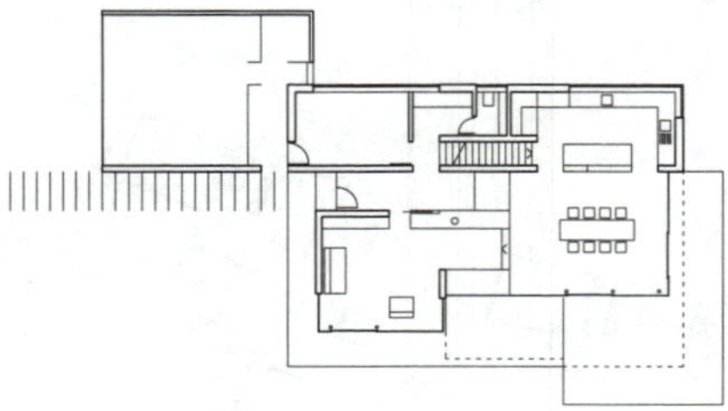

EG

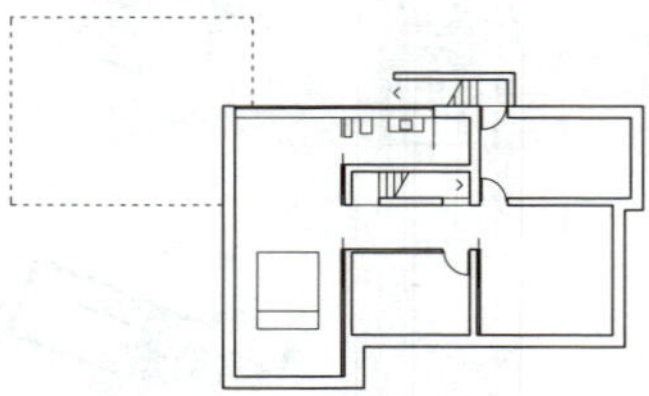

UG

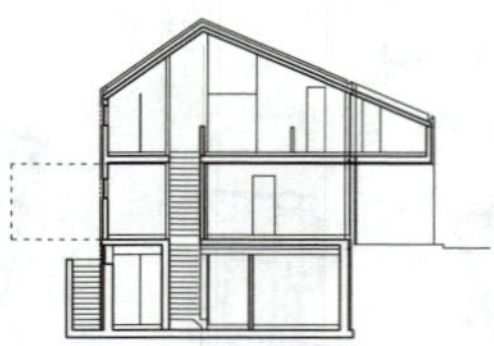

1 : 500

<234

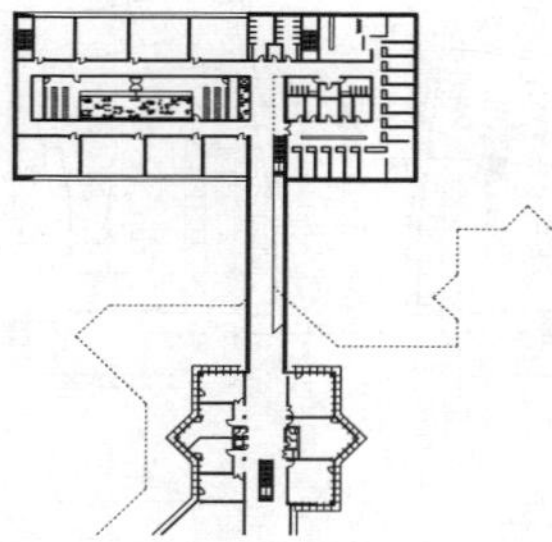

2.OG

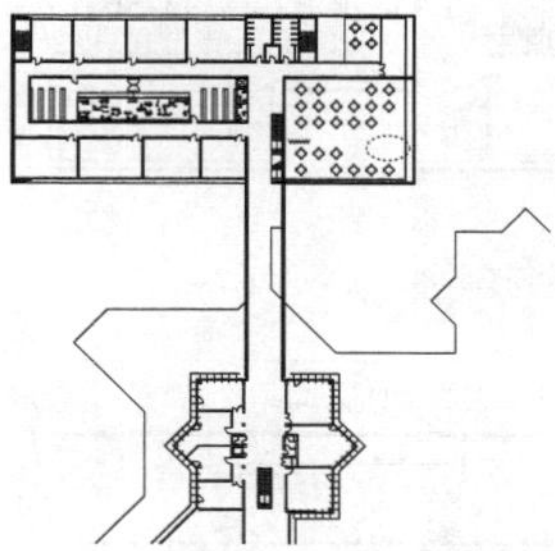

1.OG

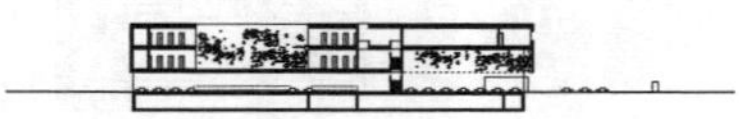

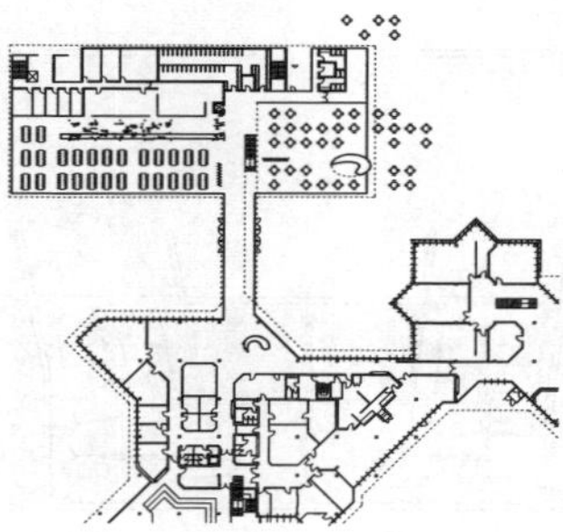

EG

DG

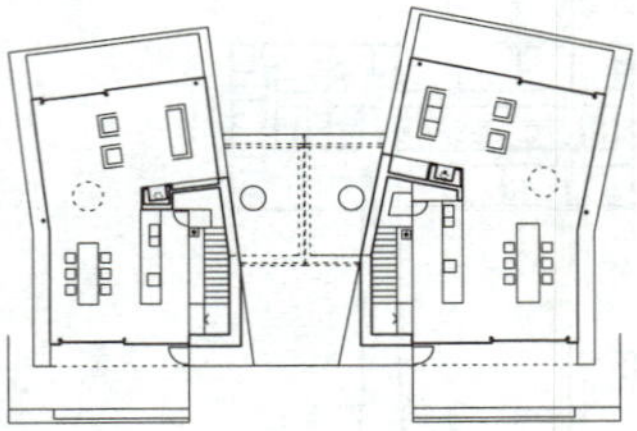

OG

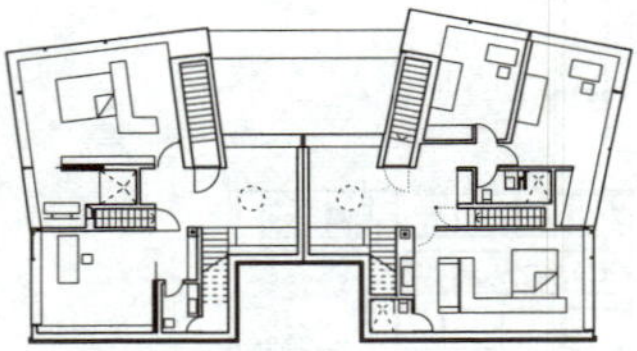

EG

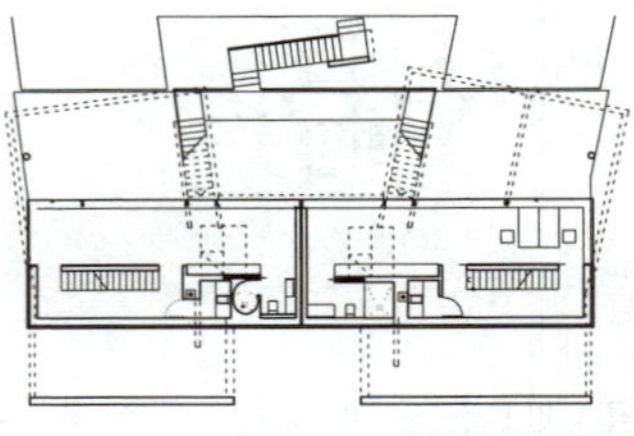

UG

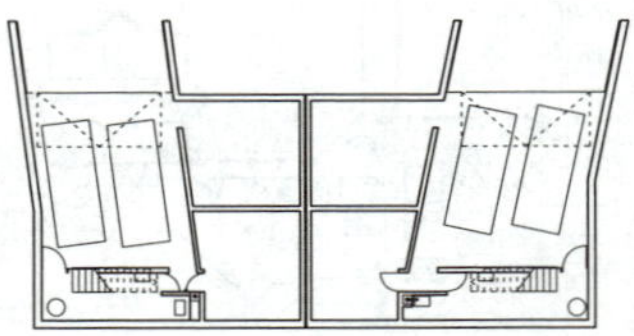

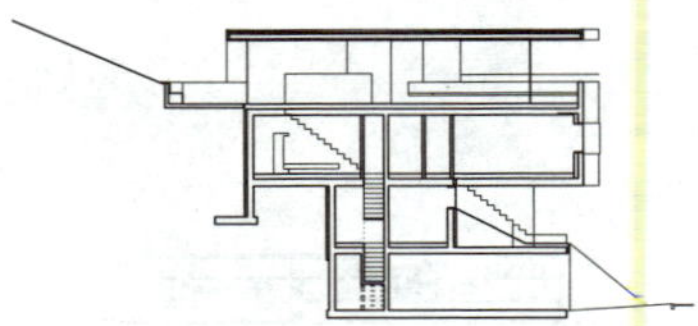

EG

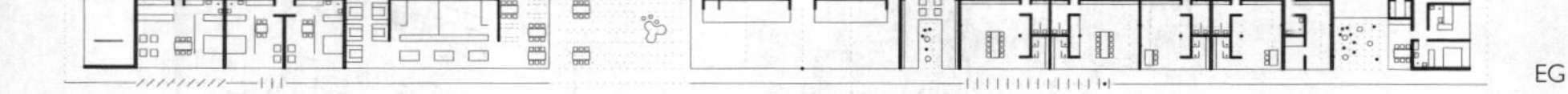

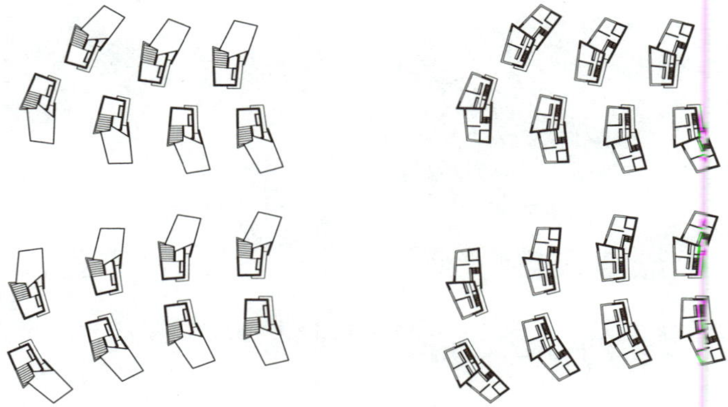

DG | OG

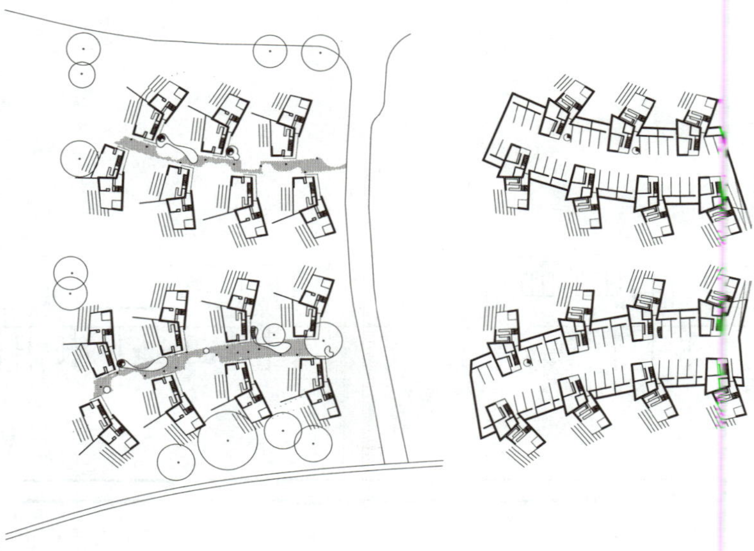

EG | KG

 <272

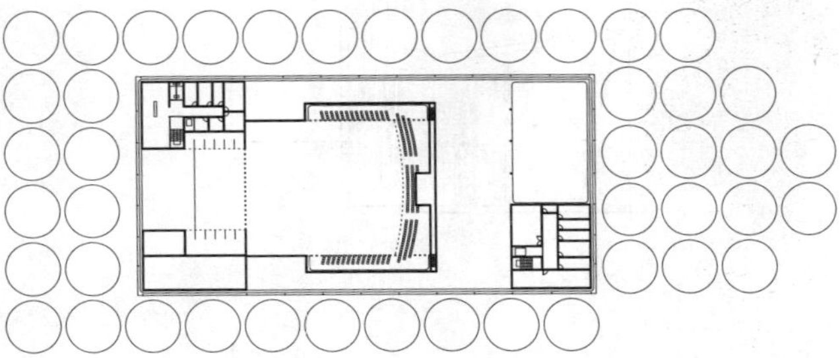

2.OG

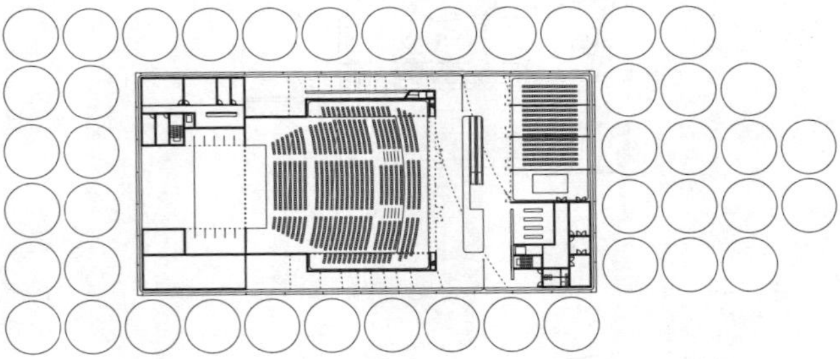

1.OG

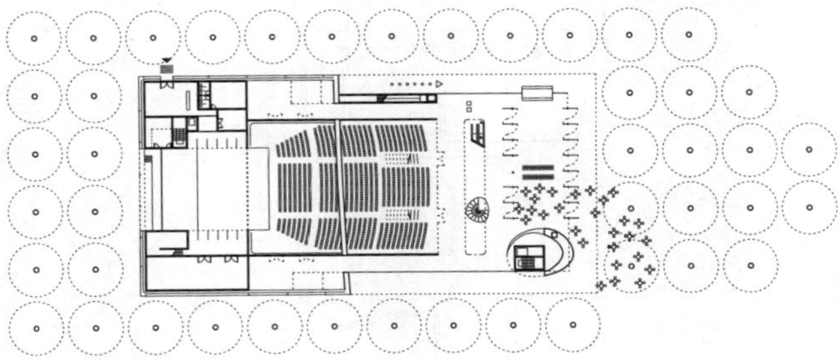

EG

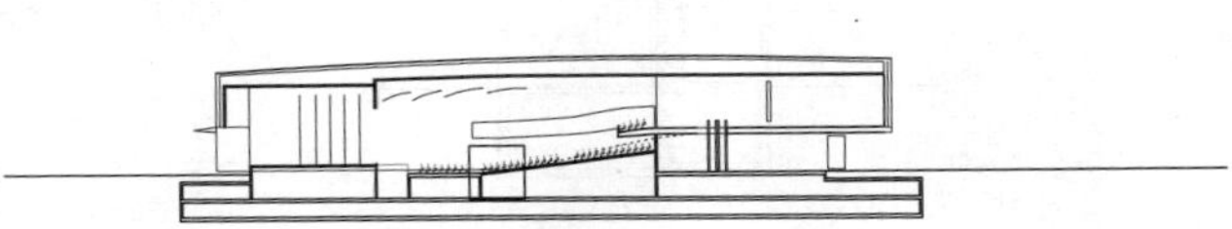

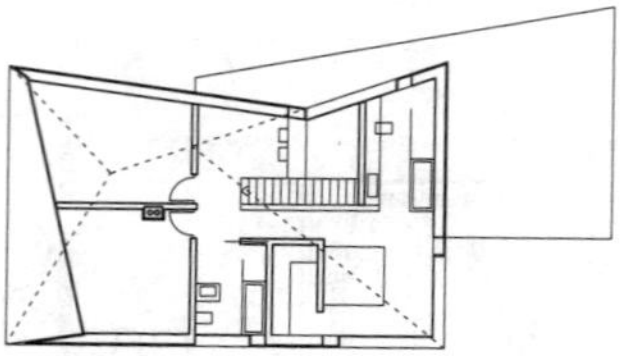

OG

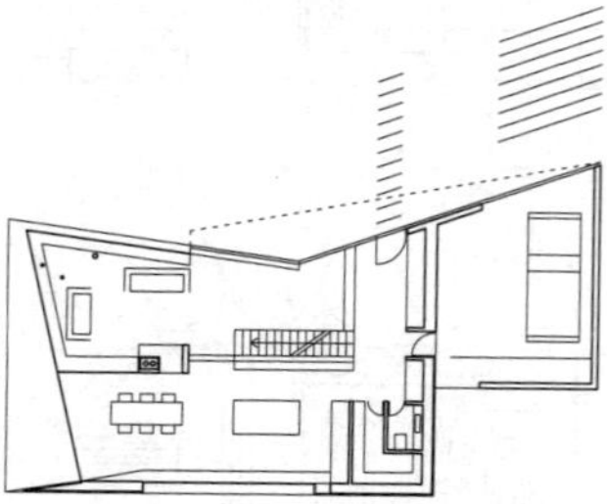

EG

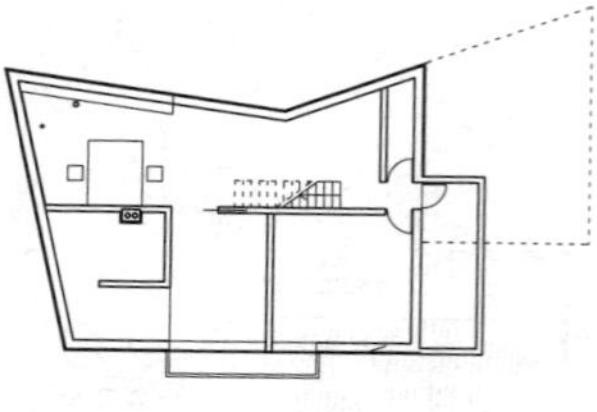

UG

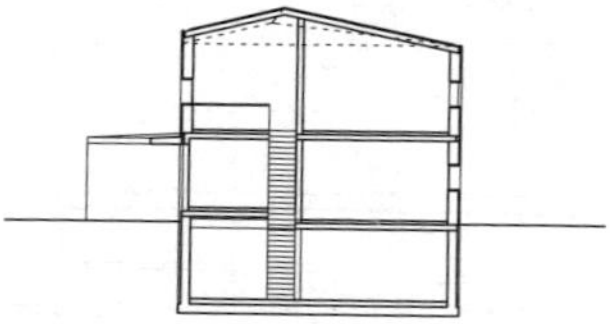

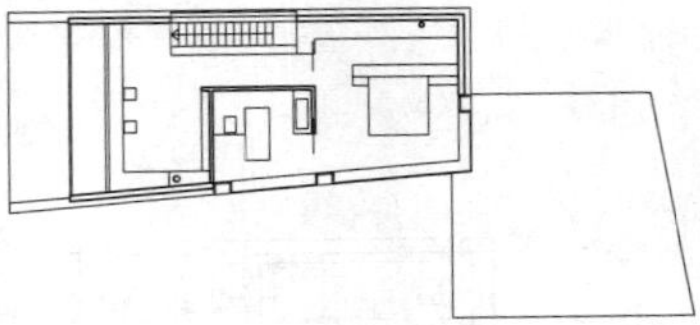

OG

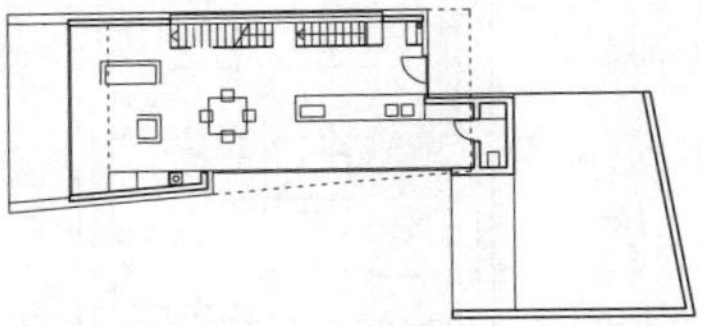

EG

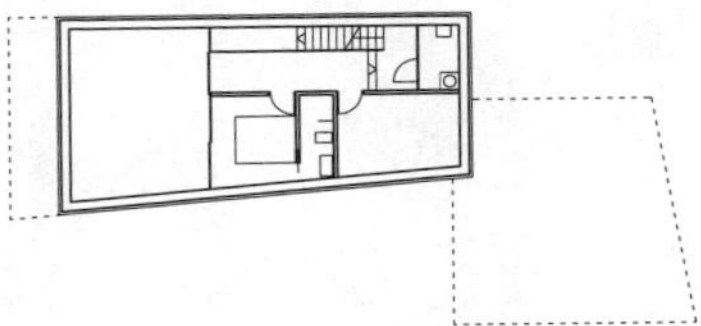

UG

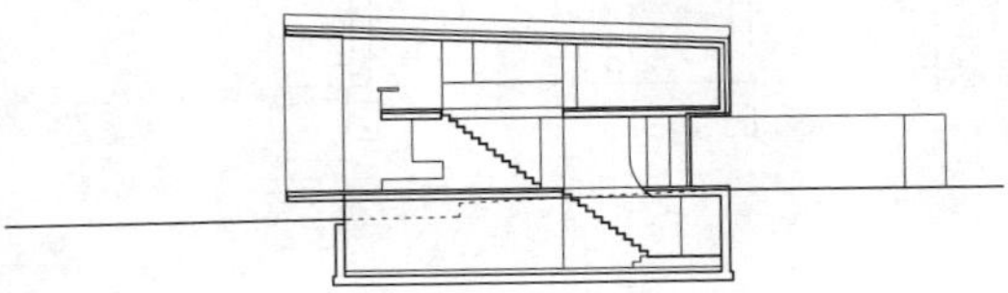

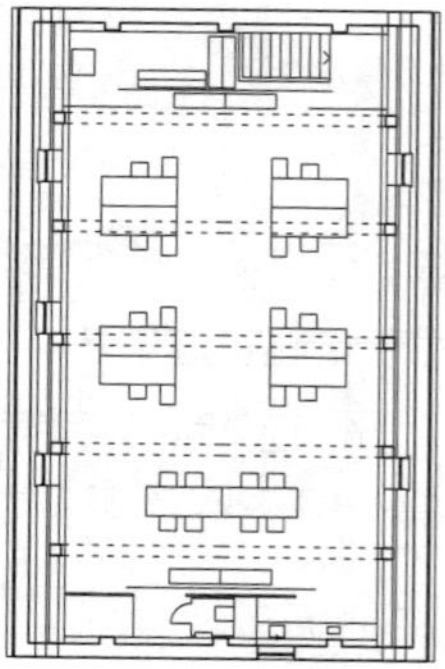

DG

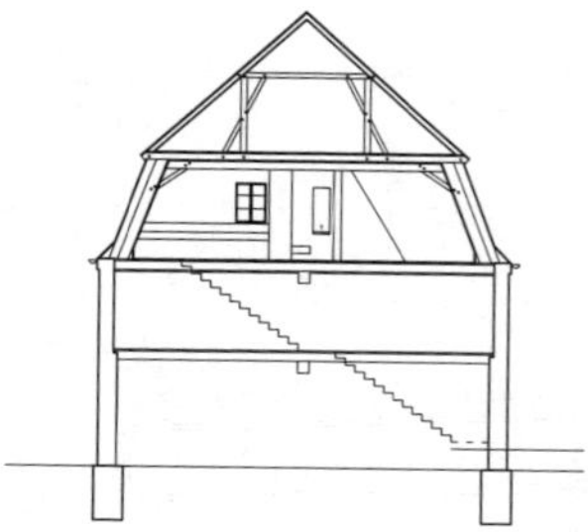

1 : 400

<306

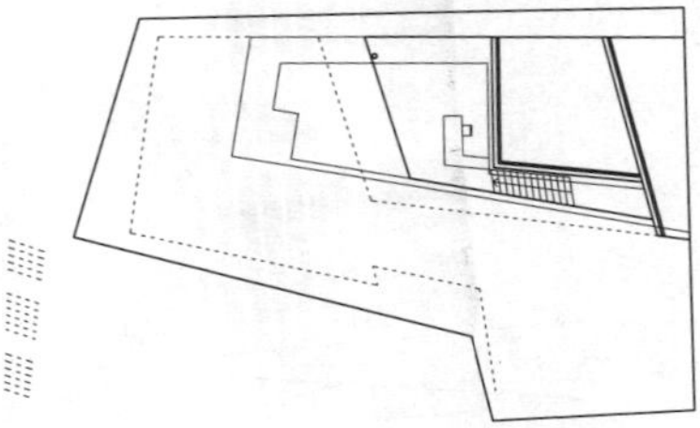

DG

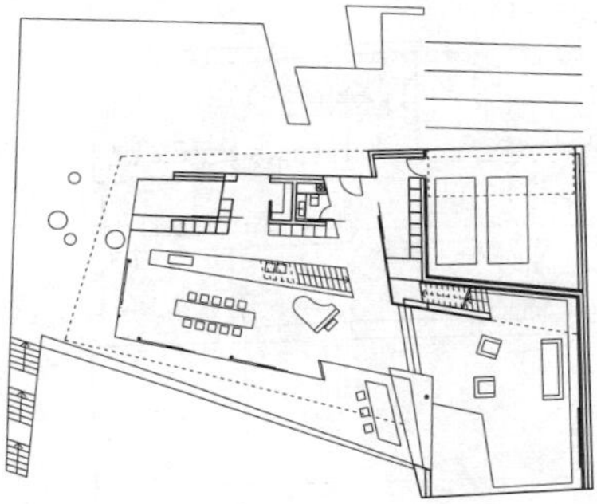

OG

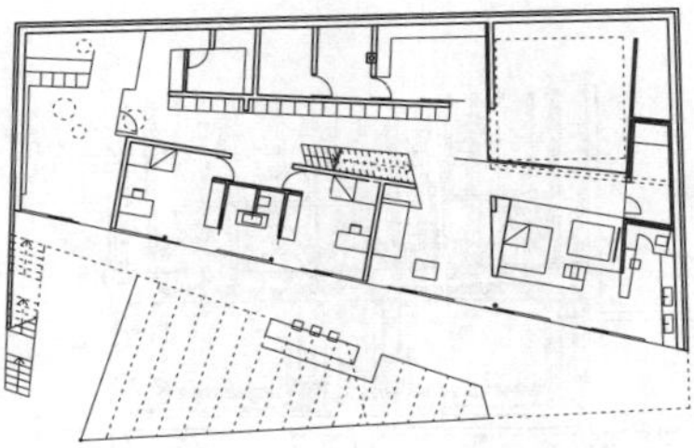

EG

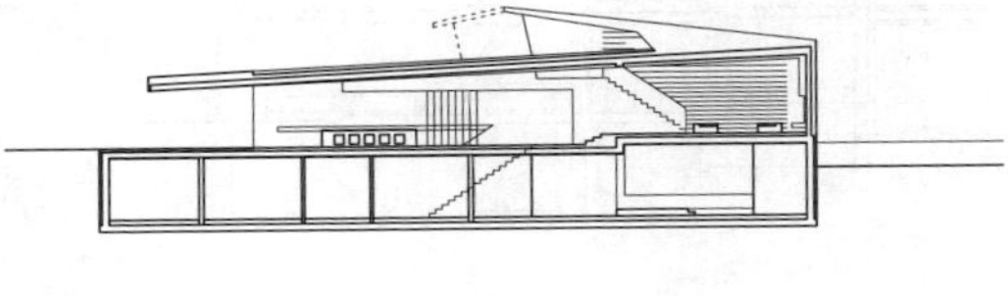

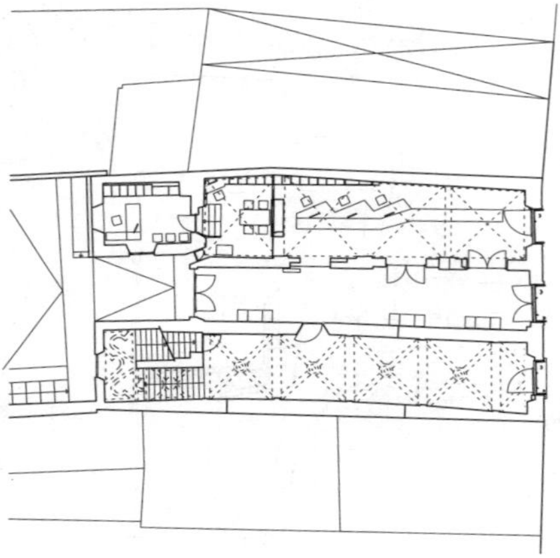

EG

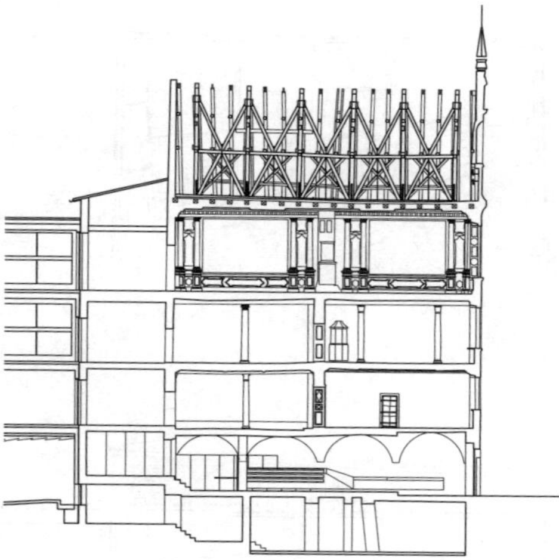

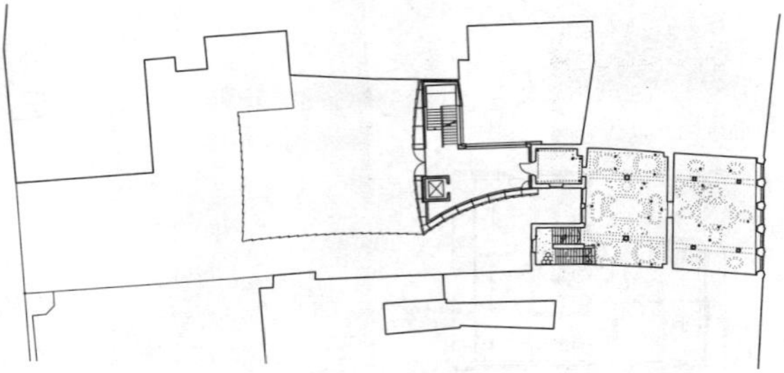

2.OG

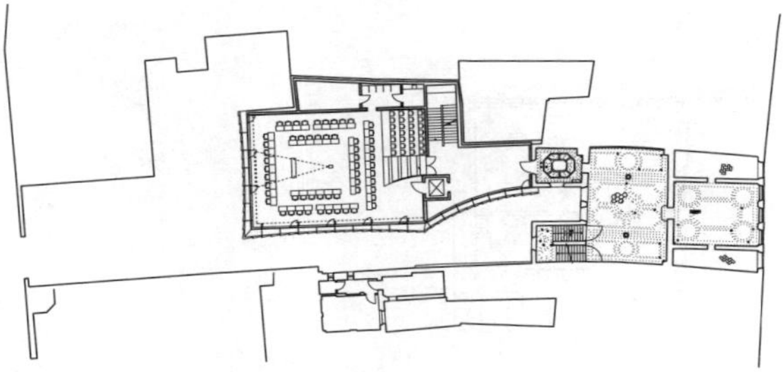

1.OG

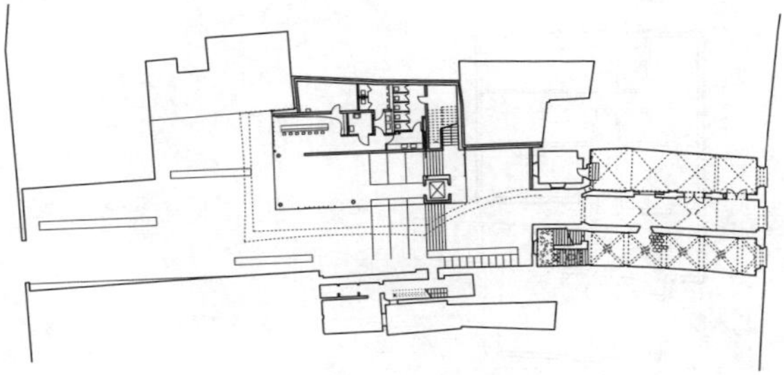

EG

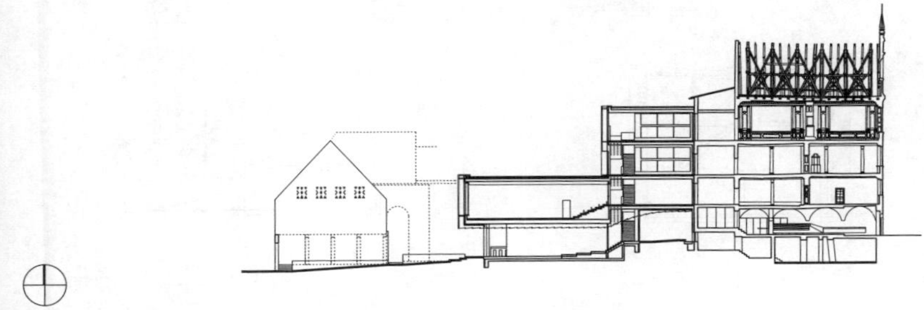

OG

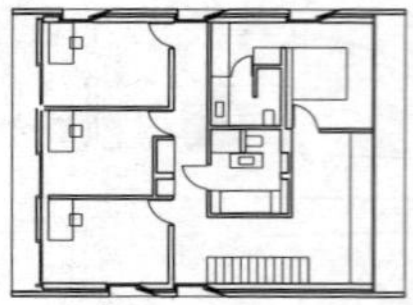

EG

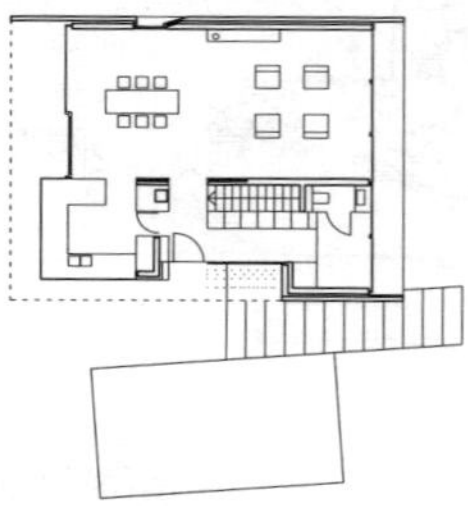

UG

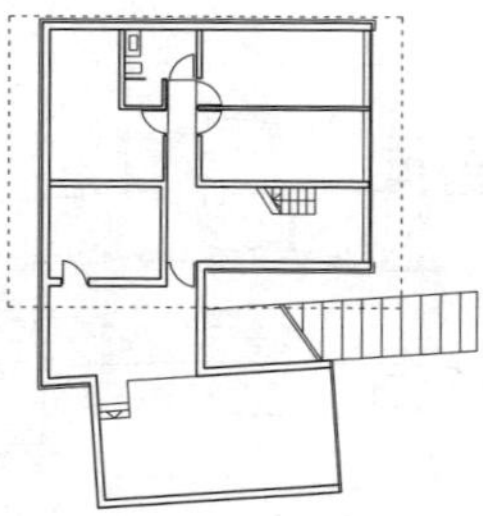

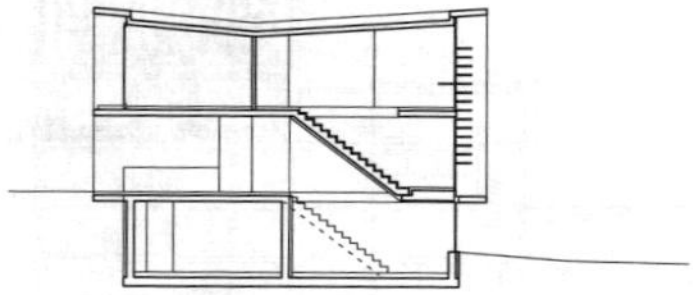

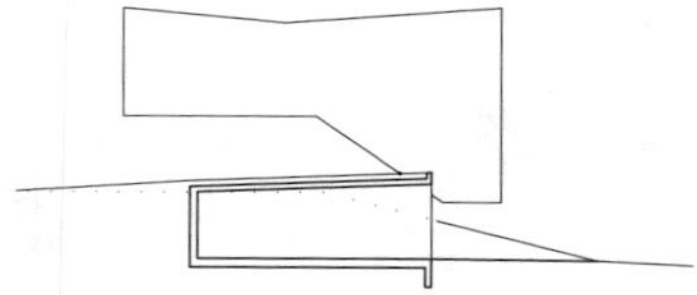

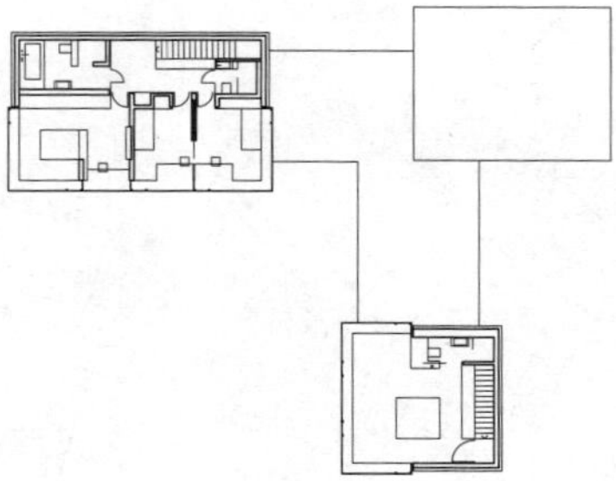

OG

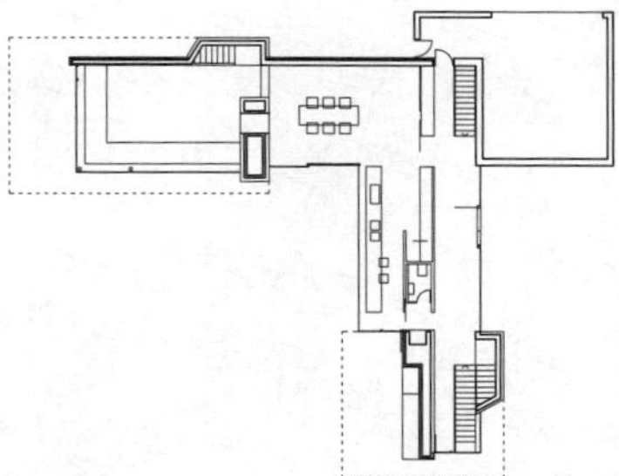

EG

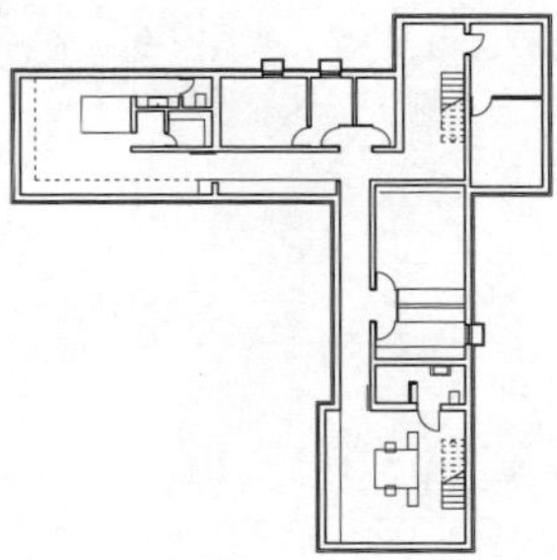

UG

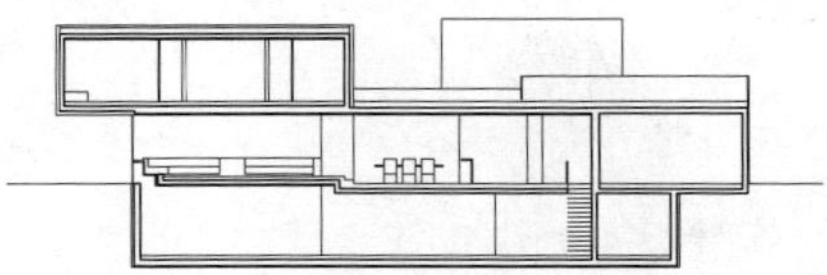

2.OG | 3.OG

EG | 1.OG

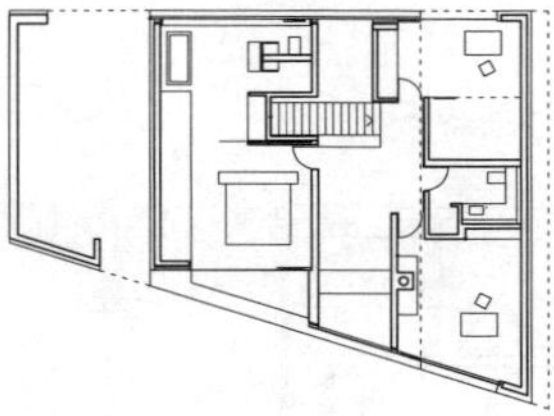

OG

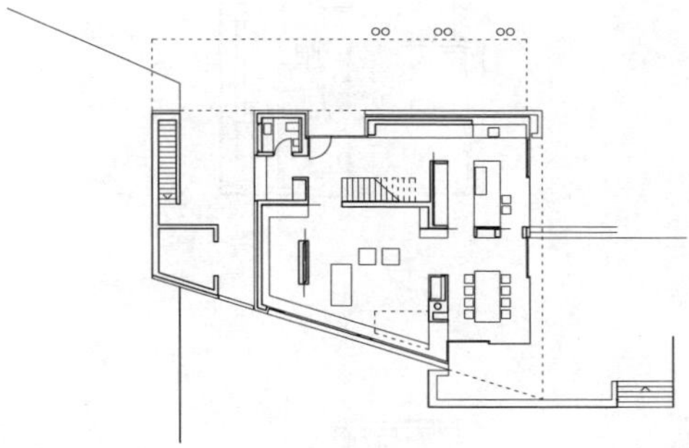

EG

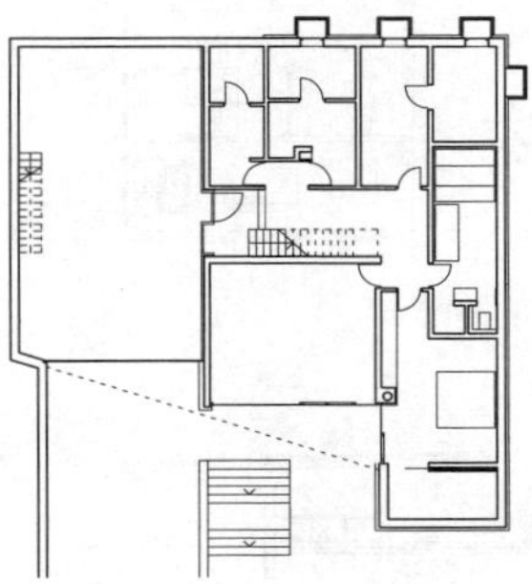

UG

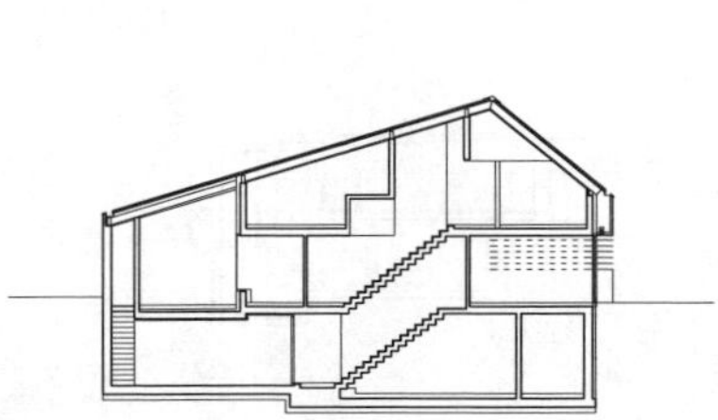

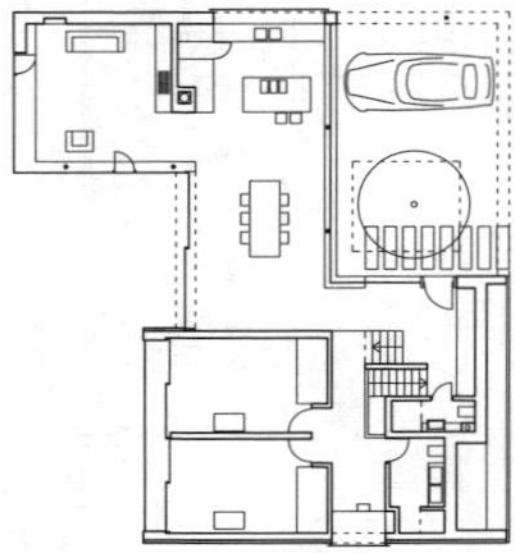

EG

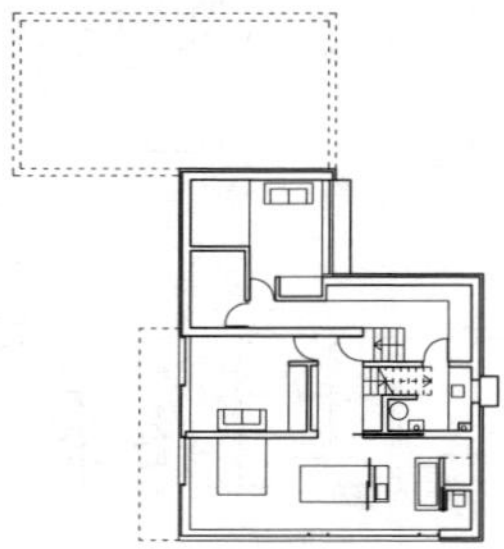

UG

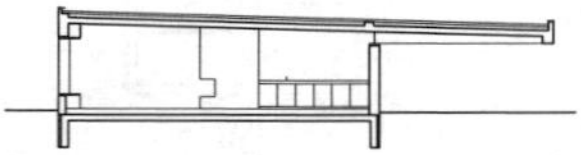

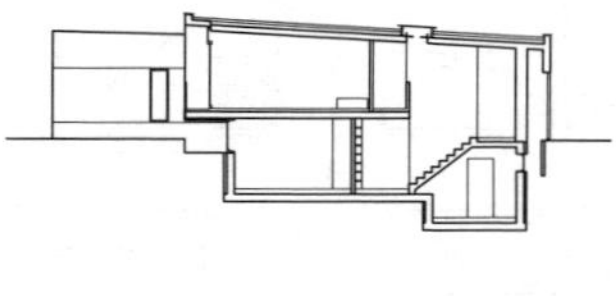

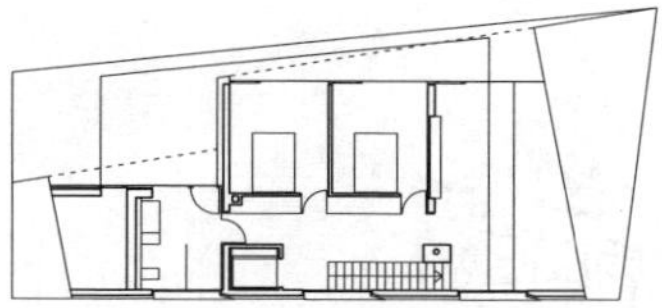

OG

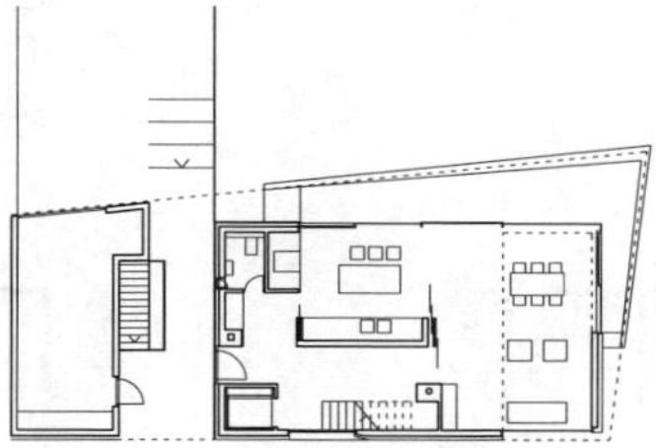

EG

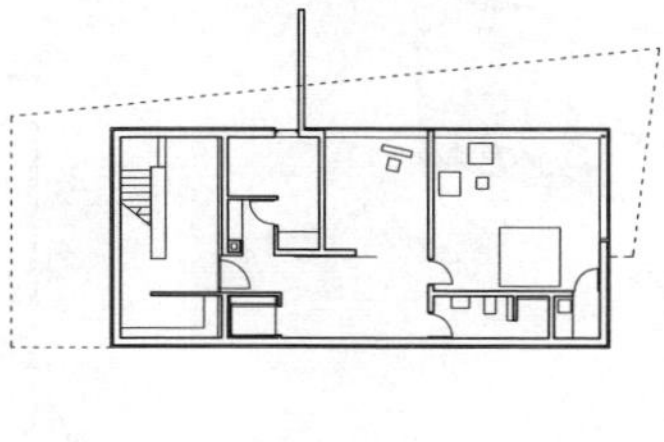

UG

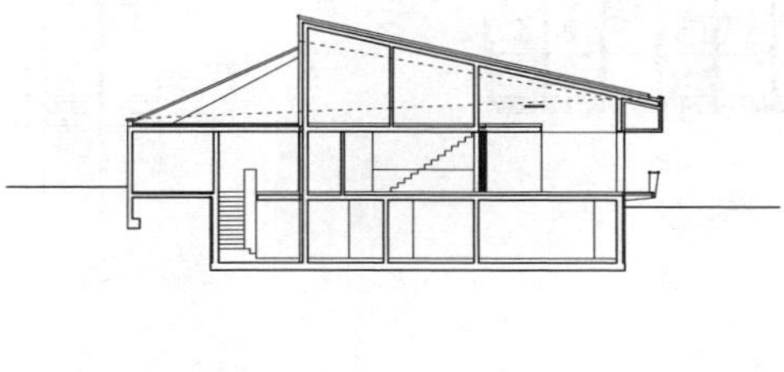

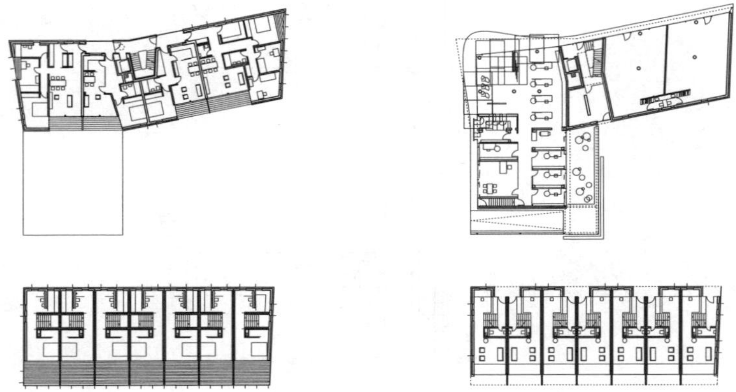

2.OG | 1.OG

EG | UG

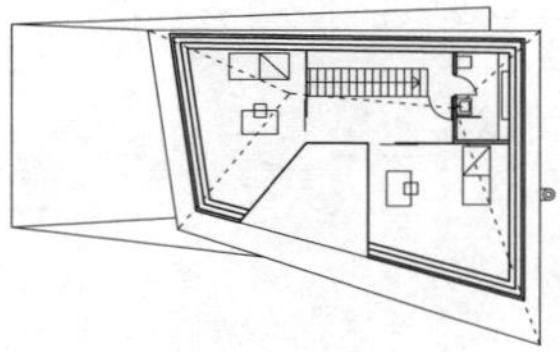

DG

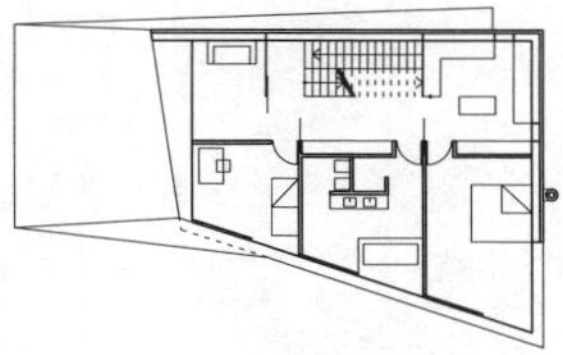

OG

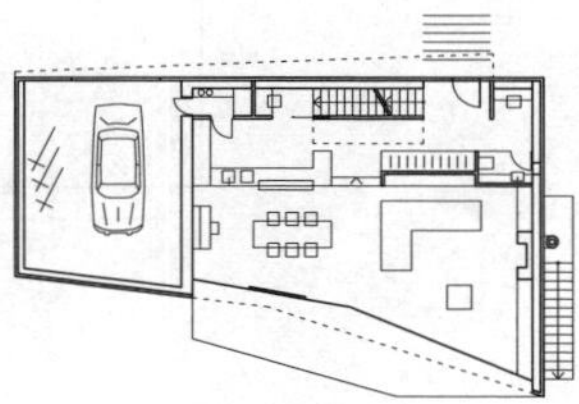

EG

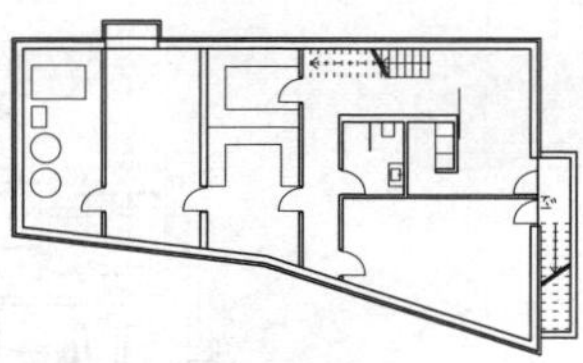

UG

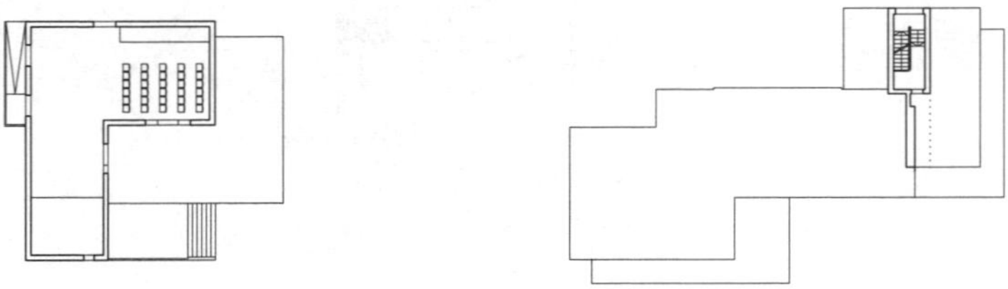

OG

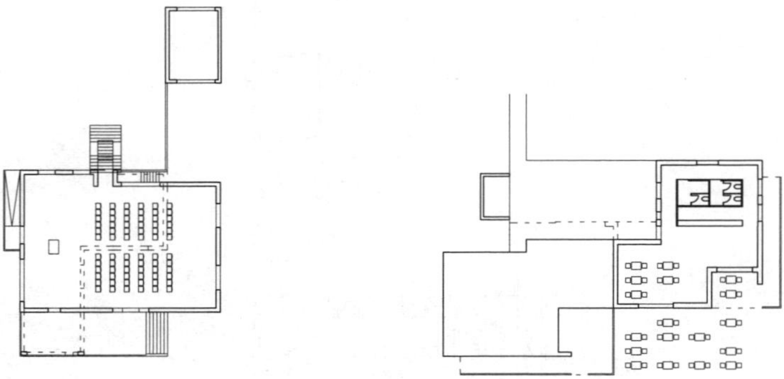

EG

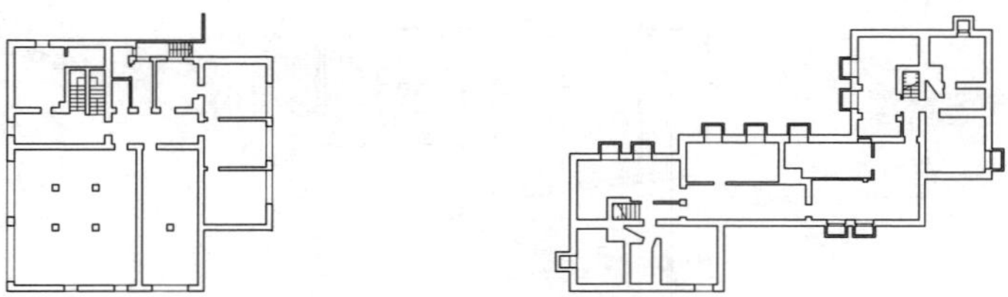

UG

1 : 700

<436

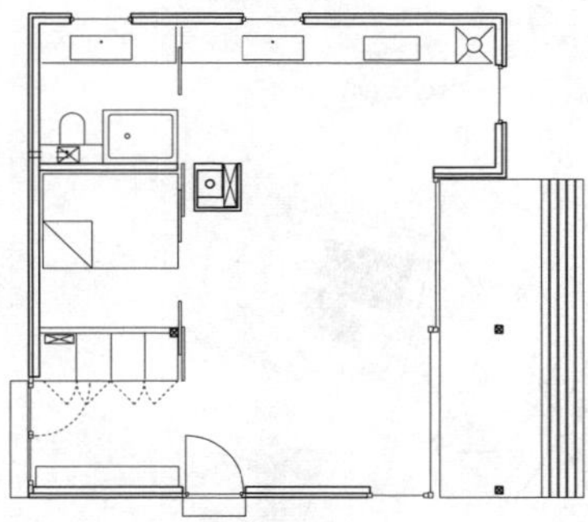

EG

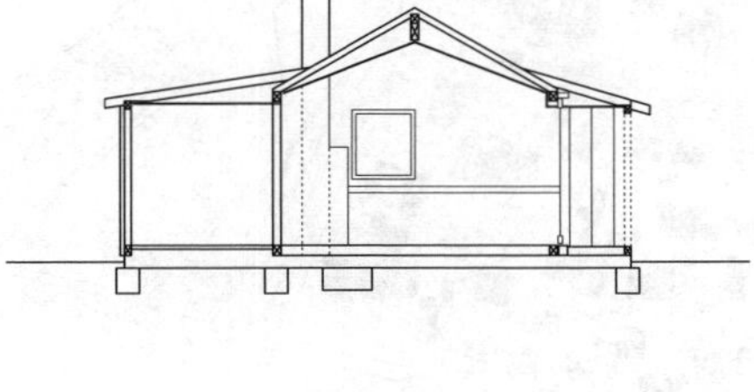

 418 SEEANLAGEN DIESSEN Diessen lake complex I : 5000 <448

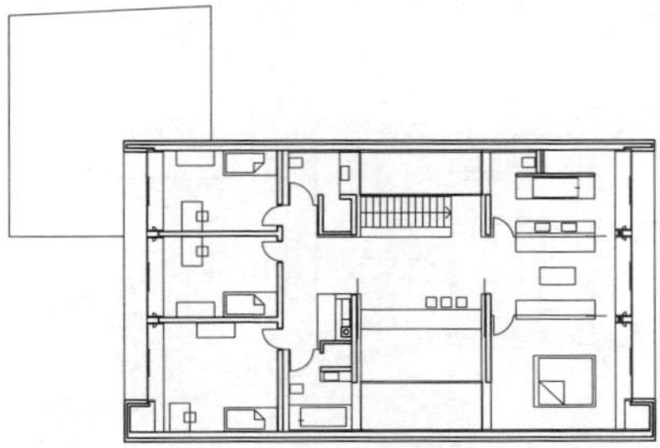

DG

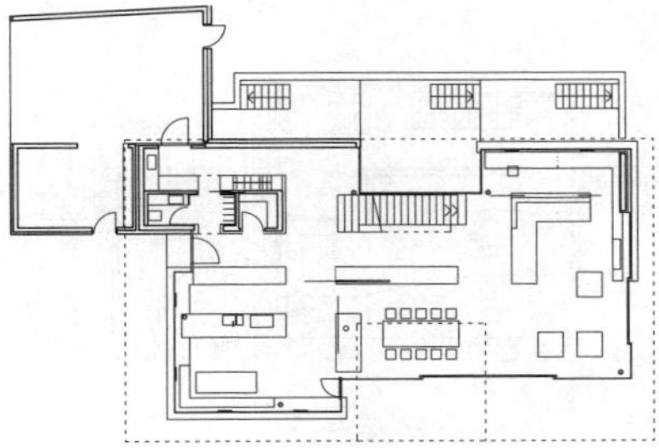

EG

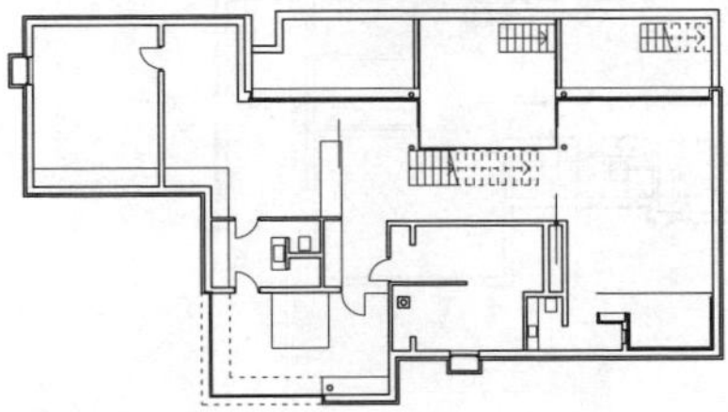

UG

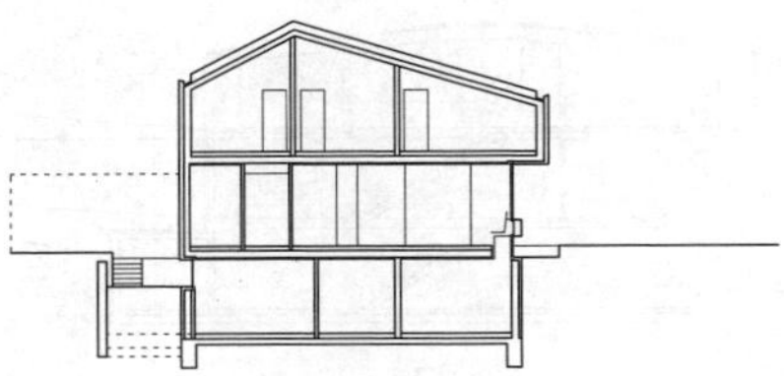

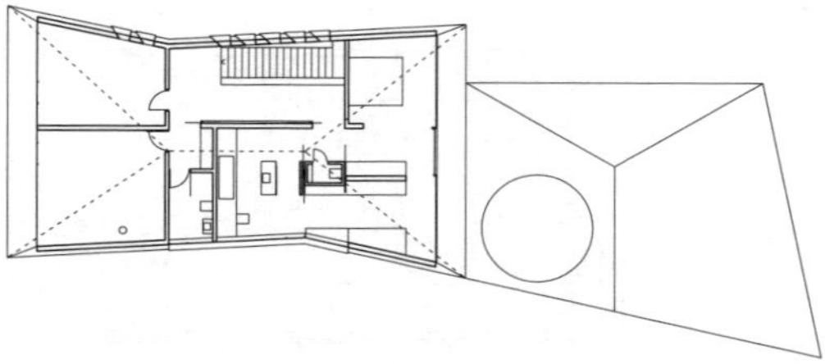

DG

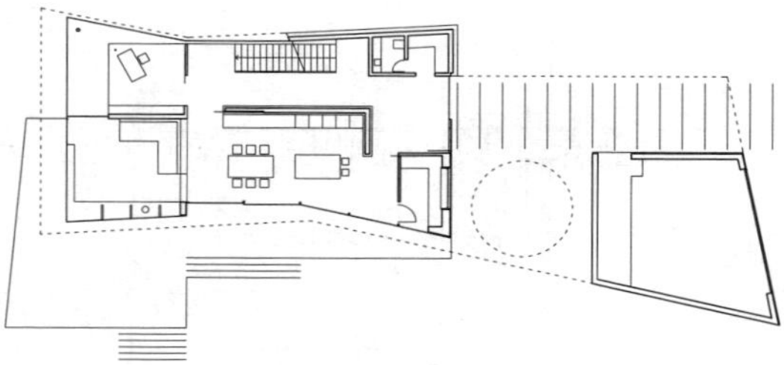

EG

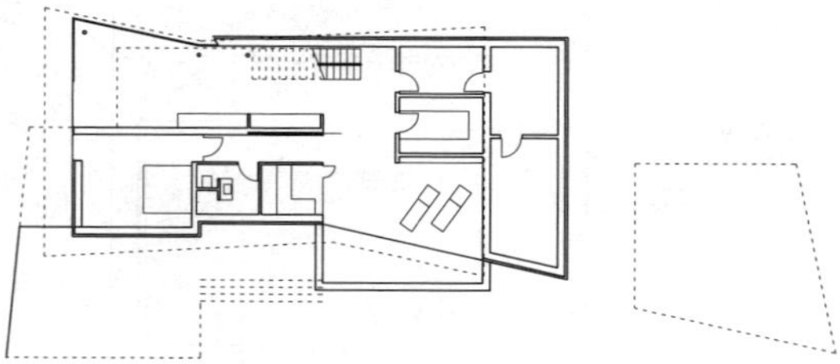

UG

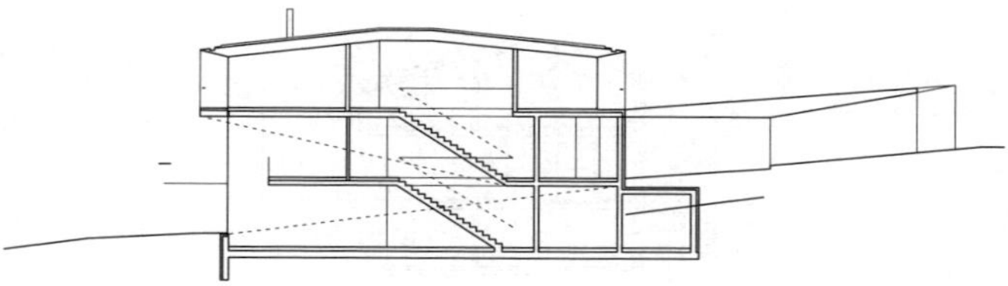

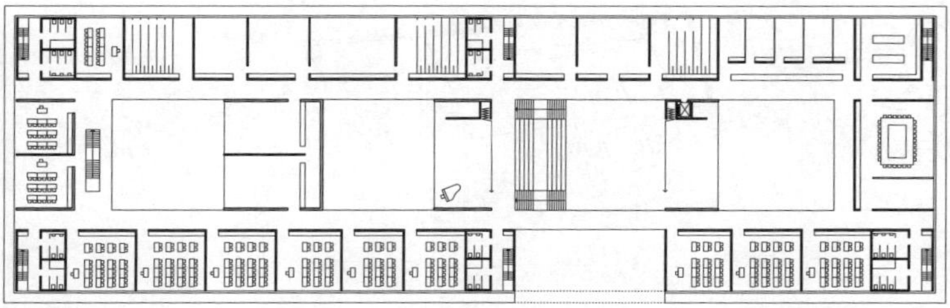

OG

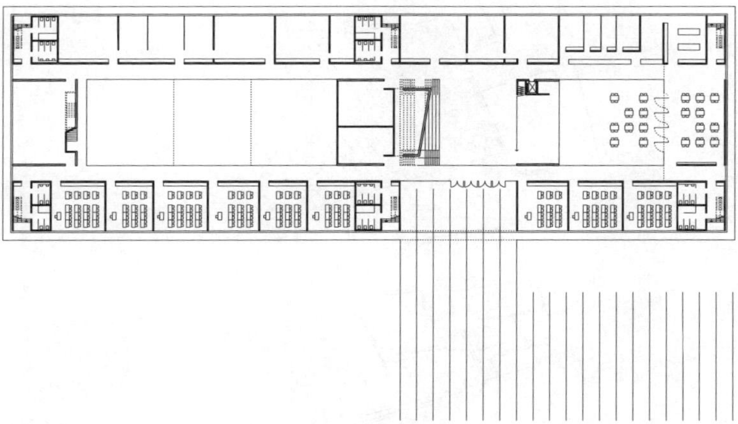

EG

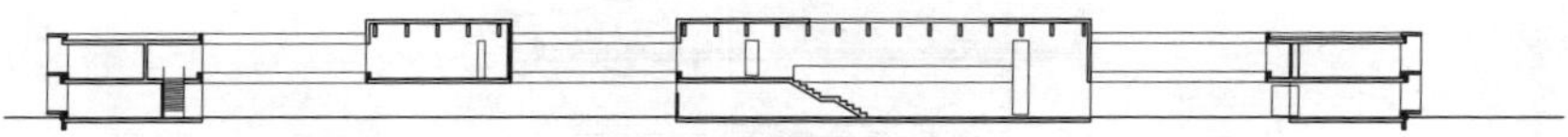

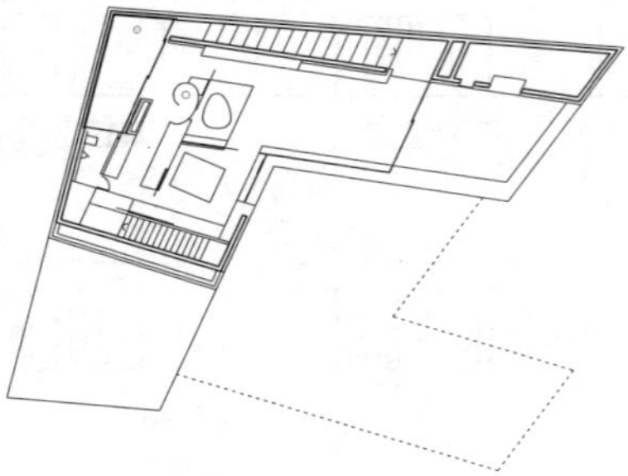

OG

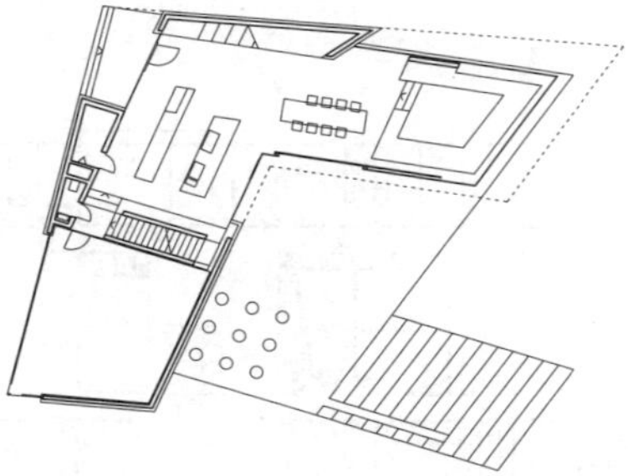

EG

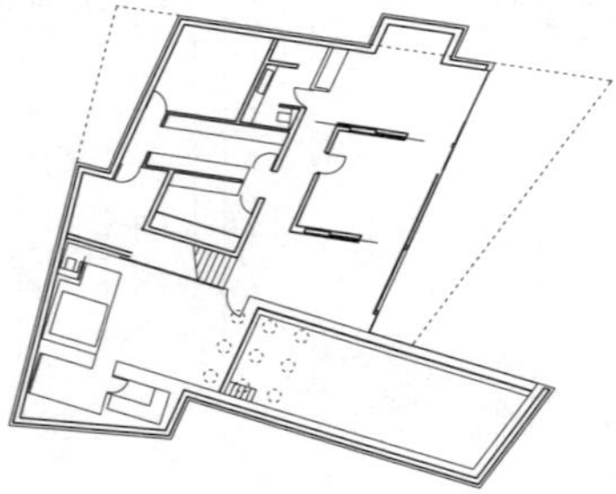

UG

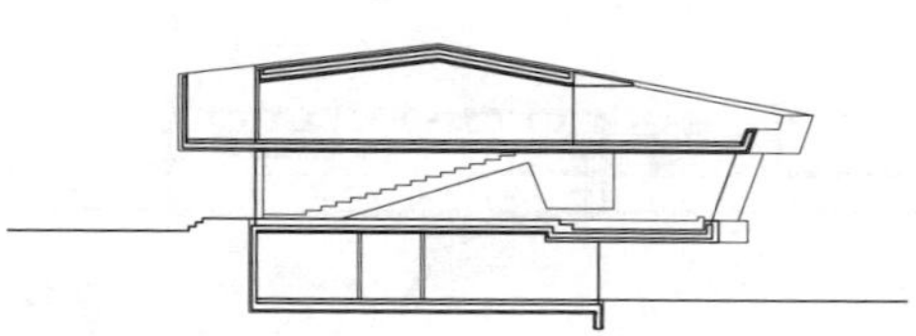

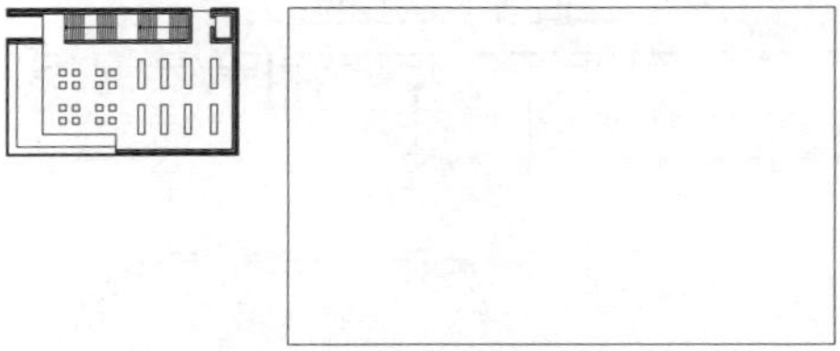

2.OG

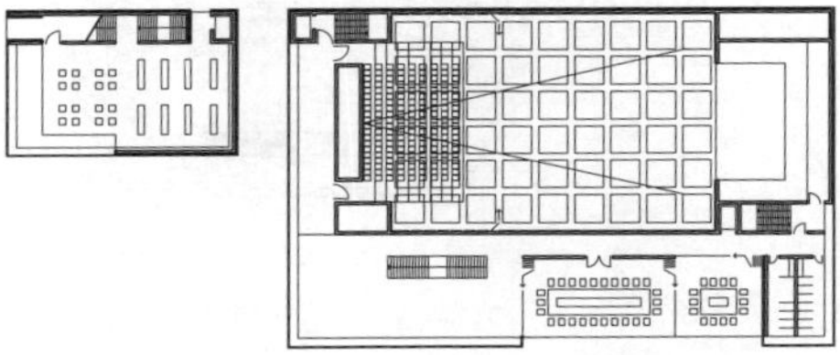

1.OG

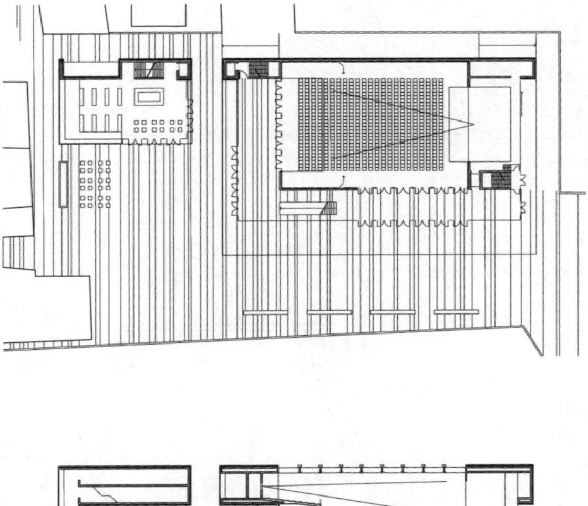

EG

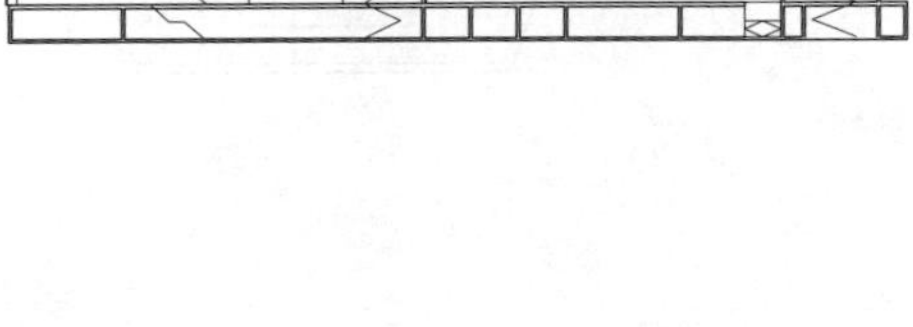

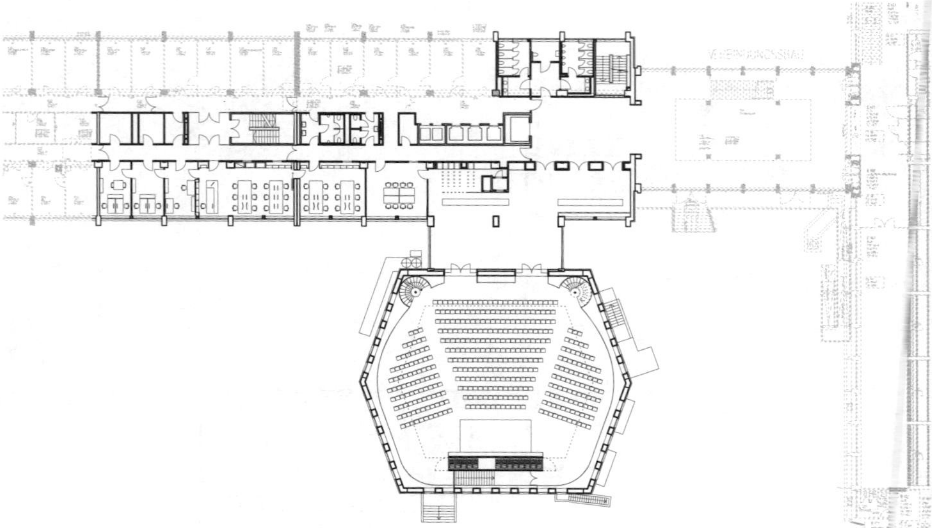
OG

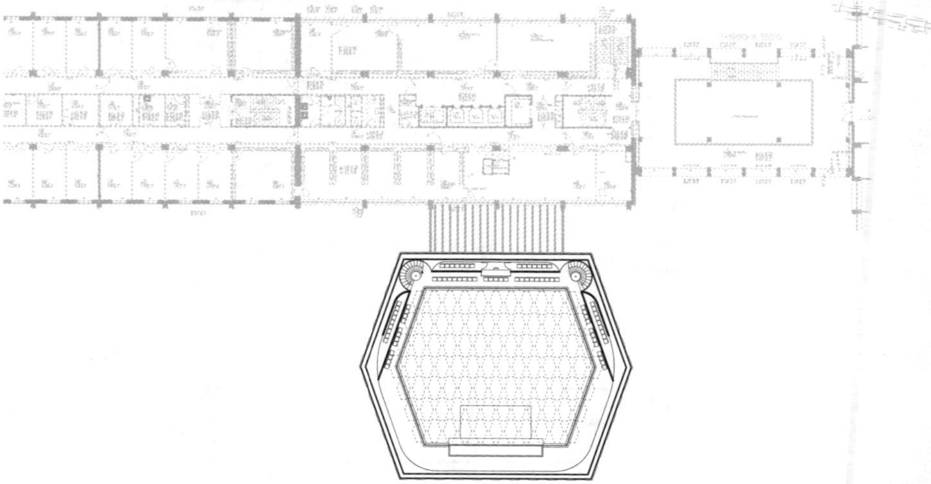
EG

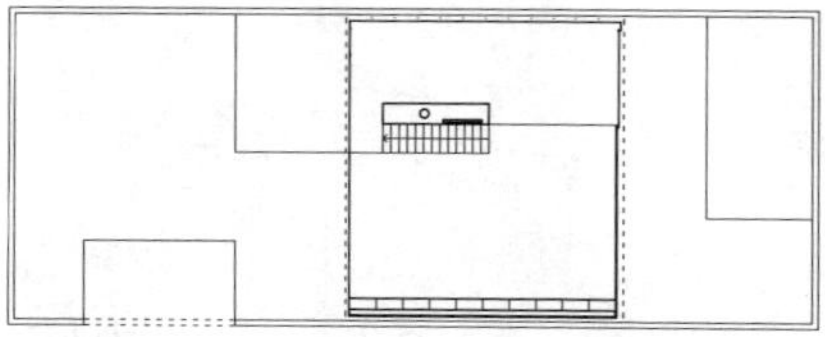

DG

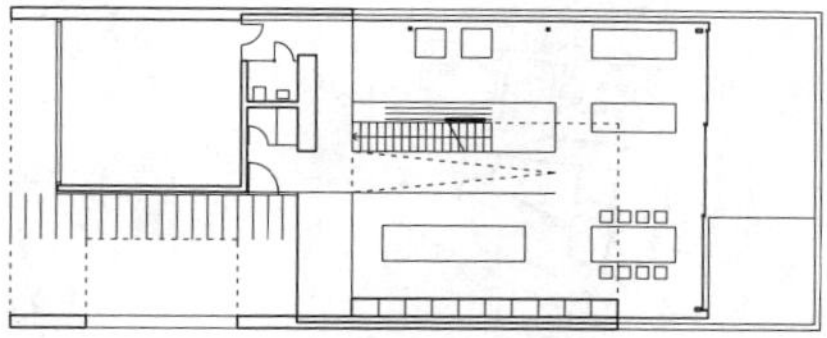

EG

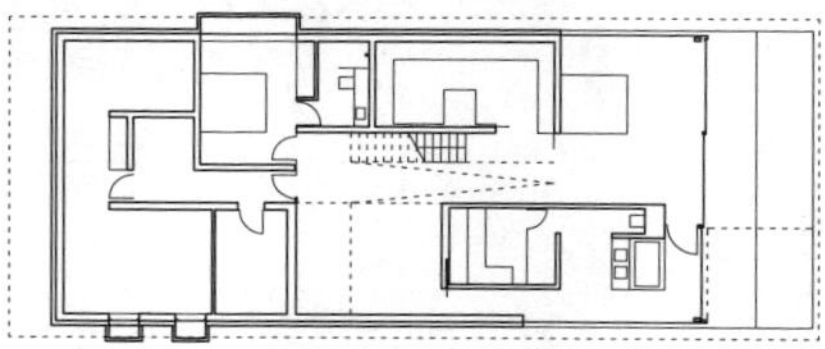

UG

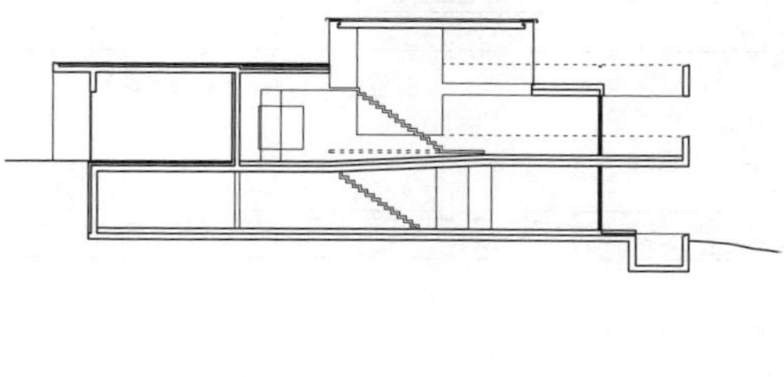

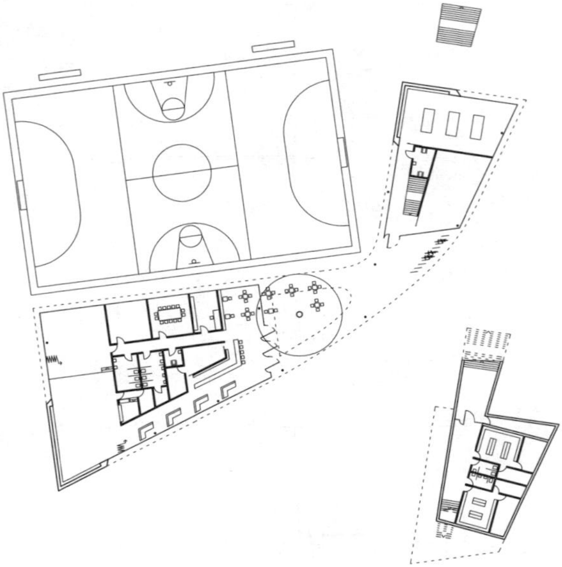

EG | UG

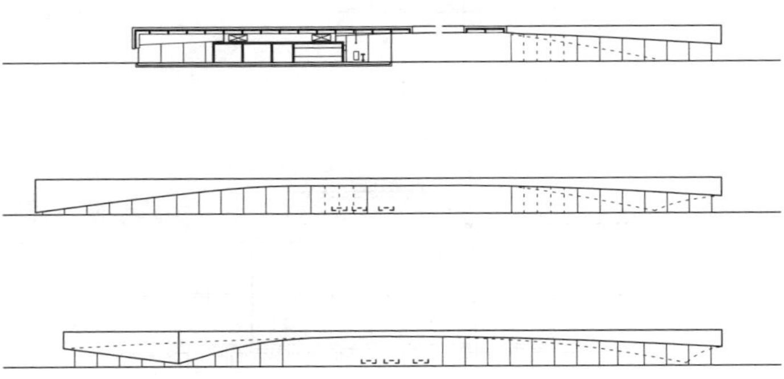

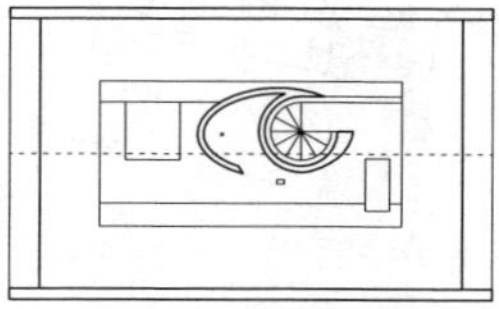

DG

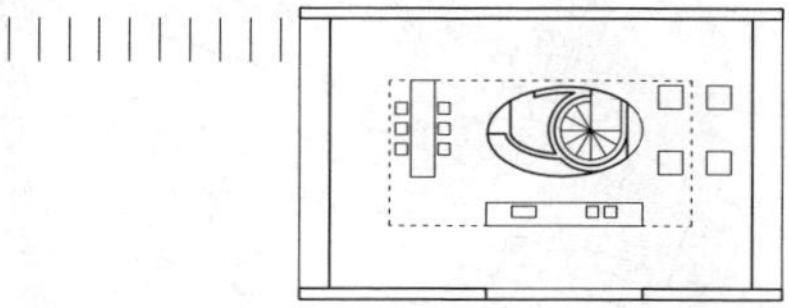

OG

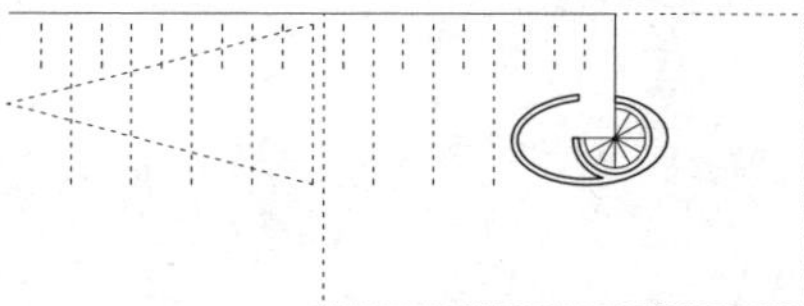

EG

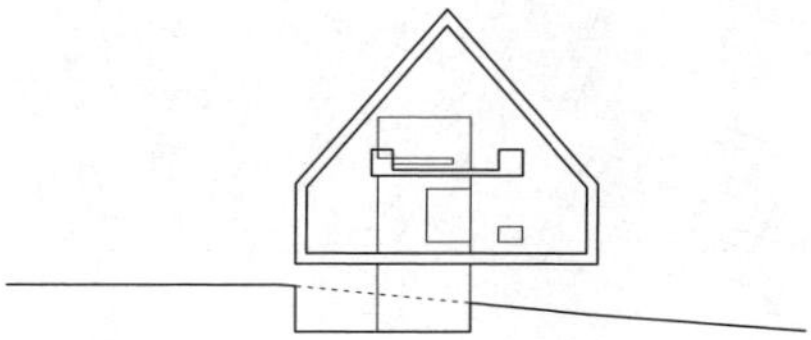

423 STÄDTEBAU „AUBING - OST“ Urban planning „Aubing - Ost“ 1 : 5000 <560

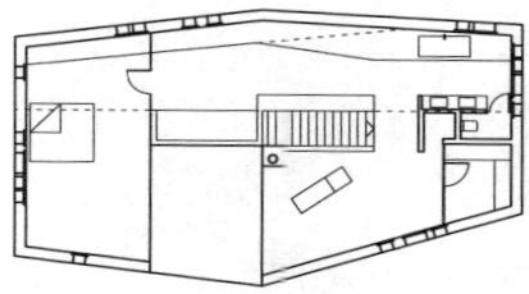

DG

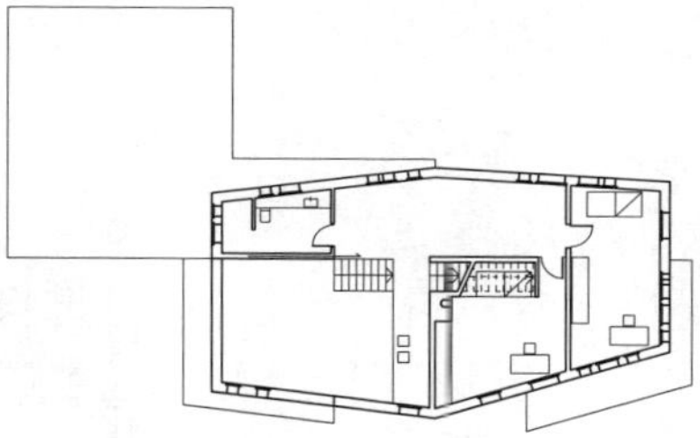

OG

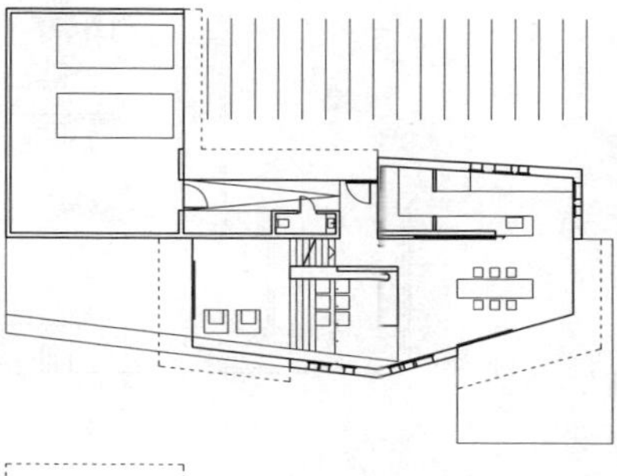

EG

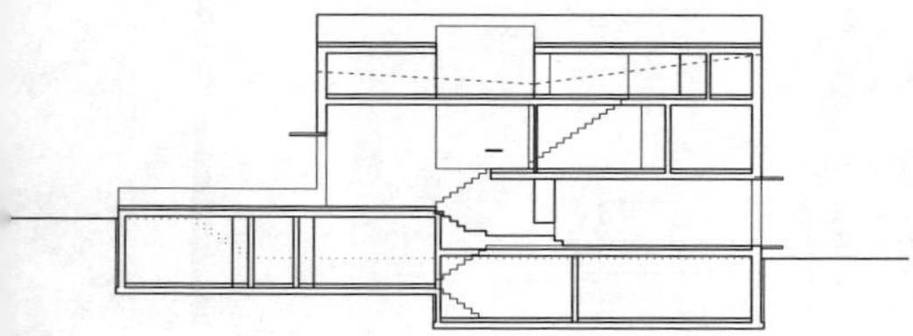

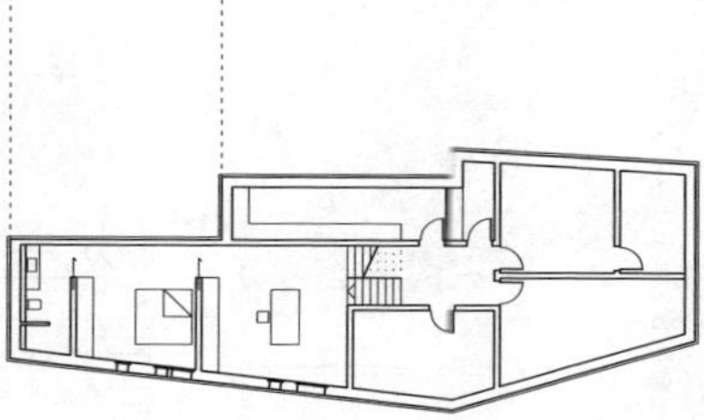

UG

<568

1:500

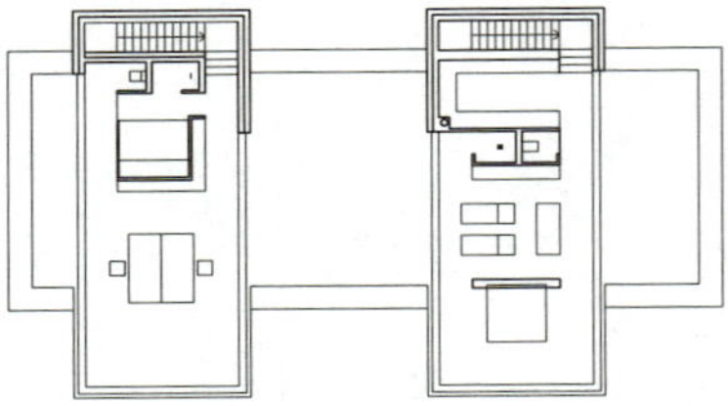

OG

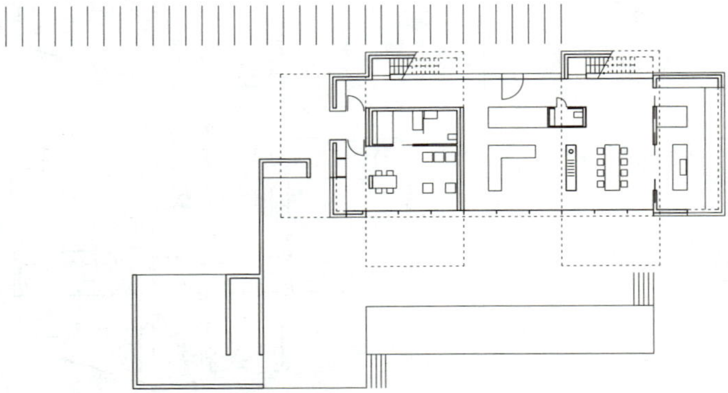

EG

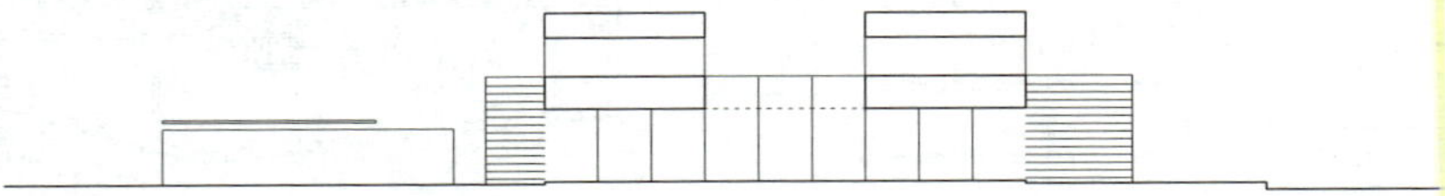

<586

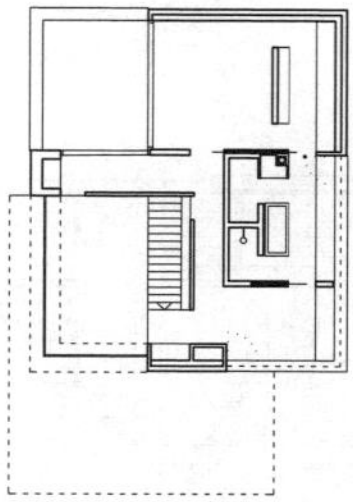

OG

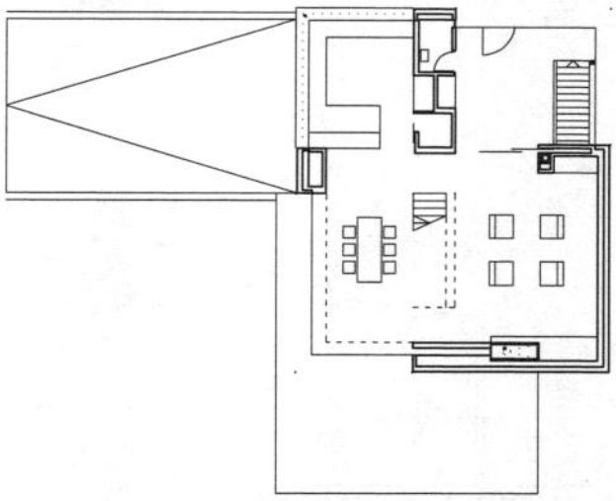

EG

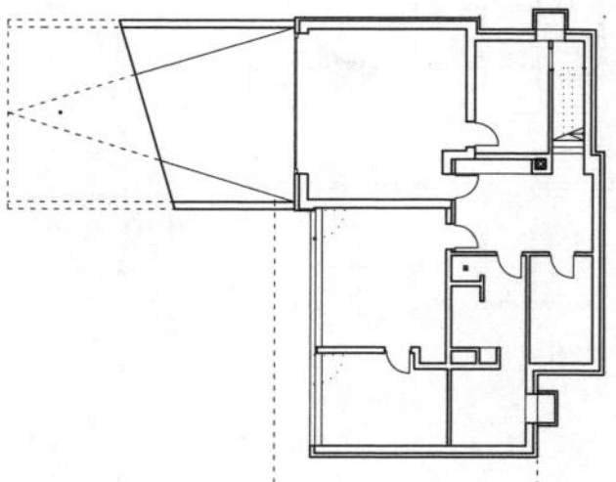

UG

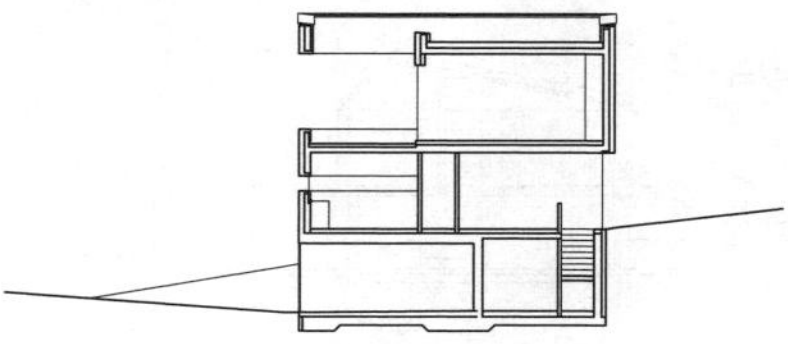

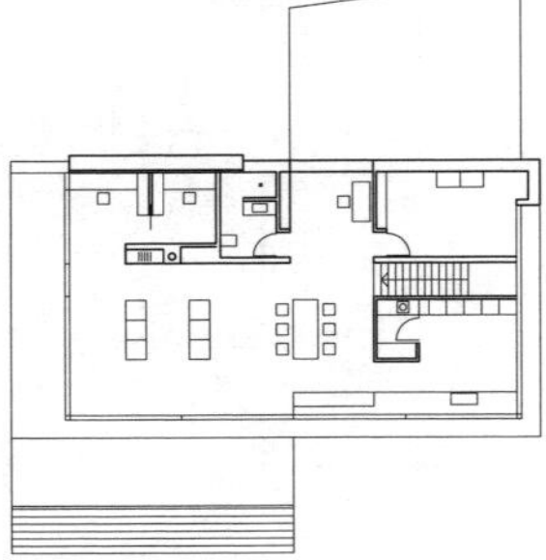

DG

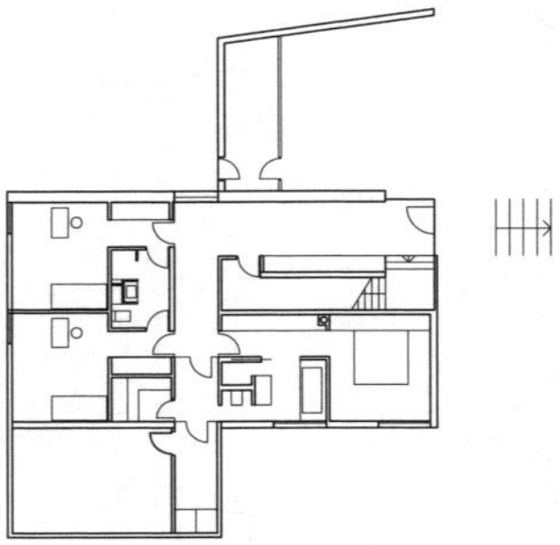

EG

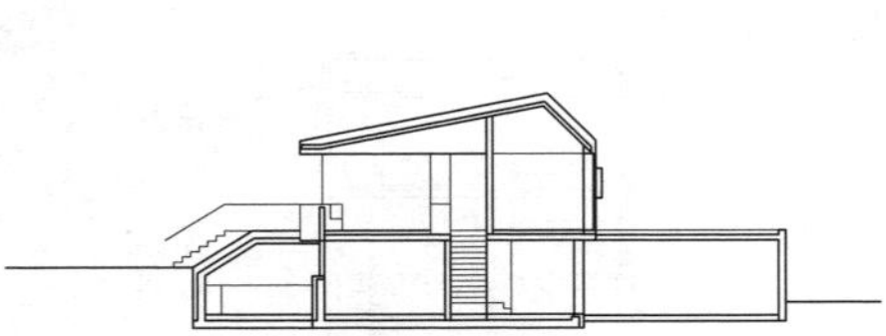

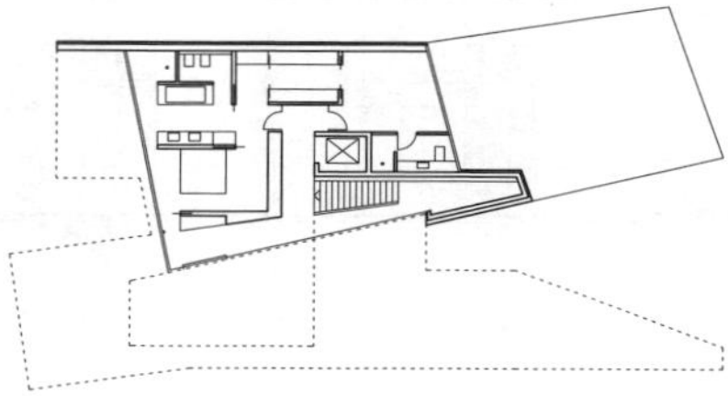

DG

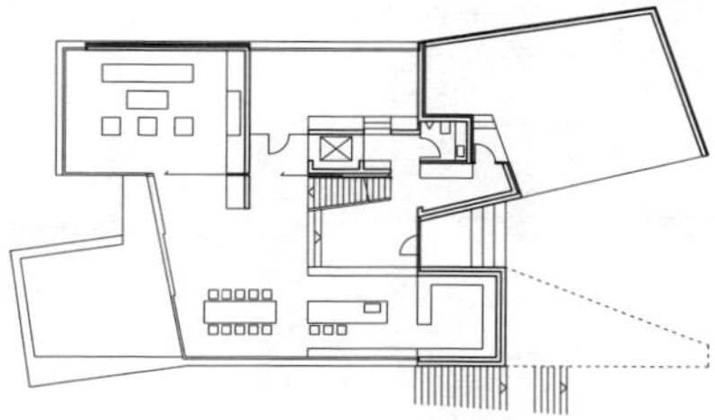

EG

UG

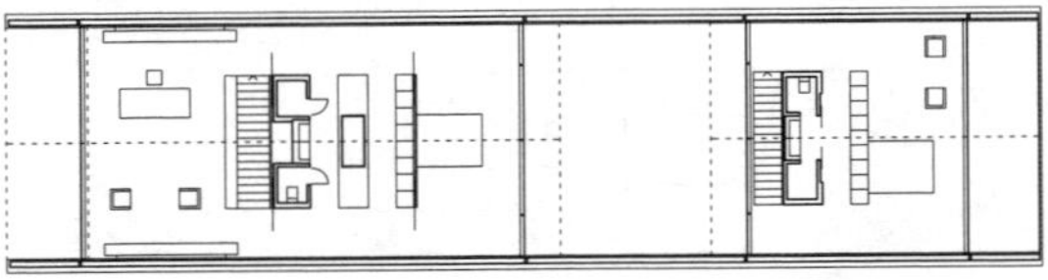

OG

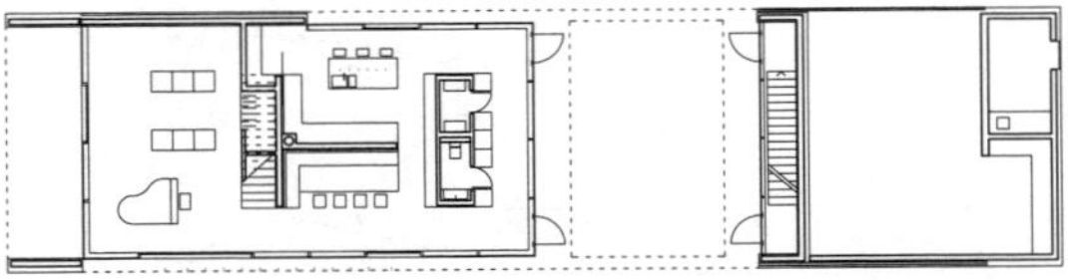

EG

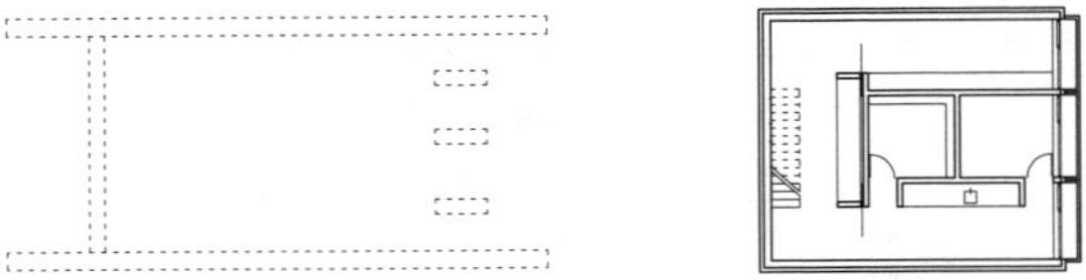

UG

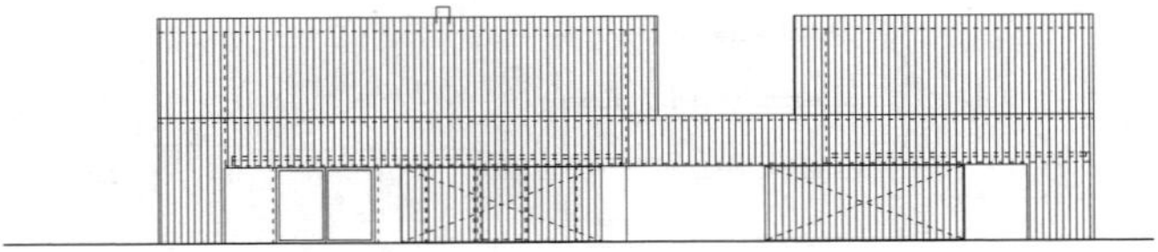

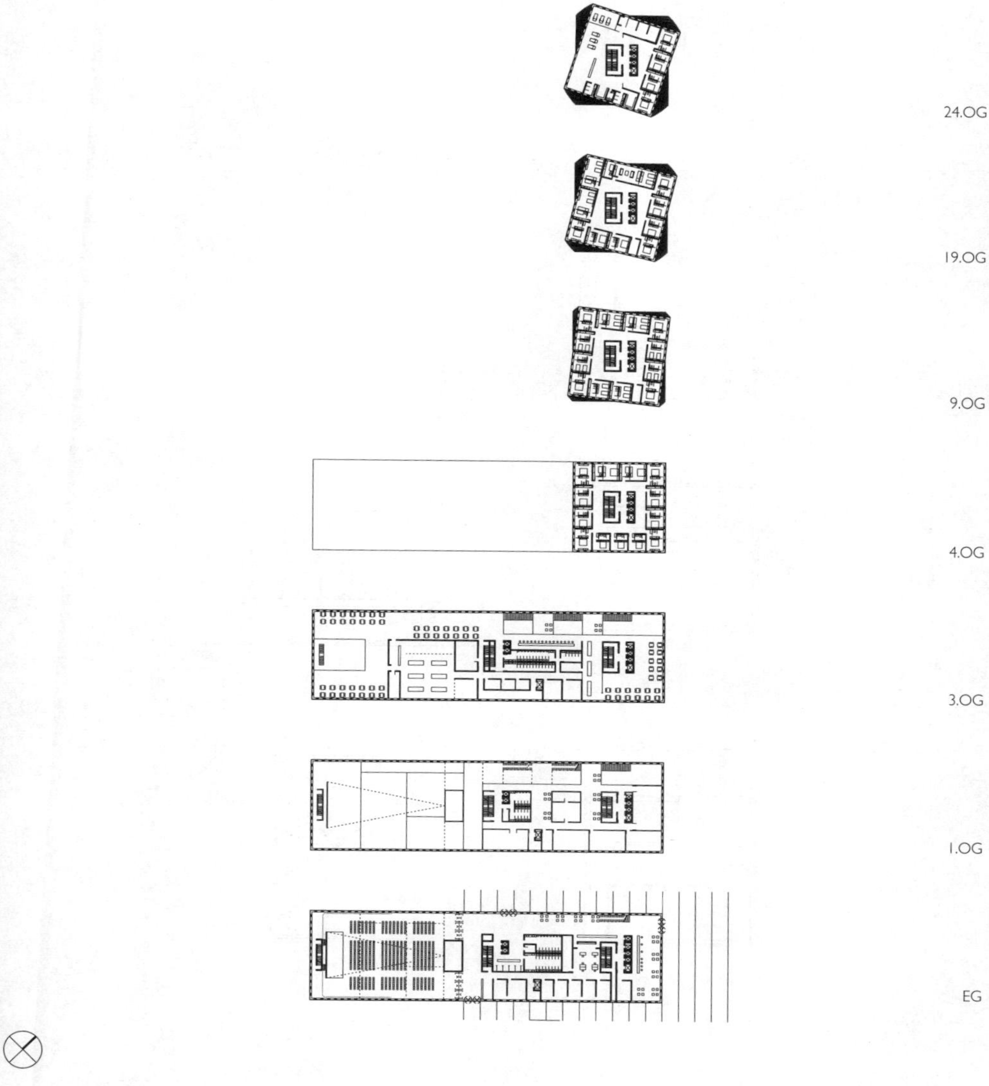
24.OG
19.OG
9.OG
4.OG
3.OG
1.OG
EG

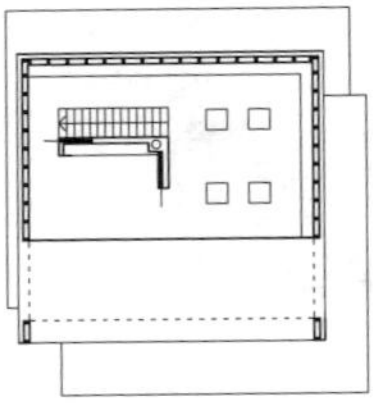

DG

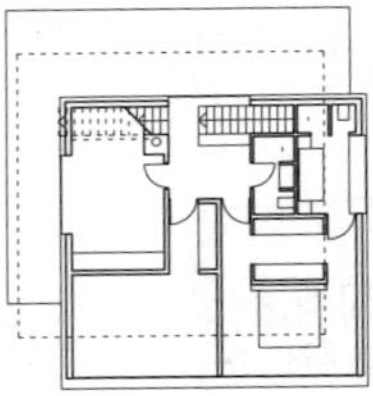

OG

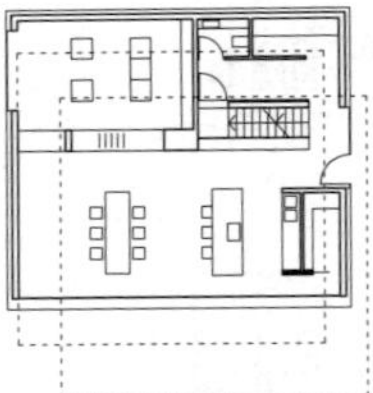

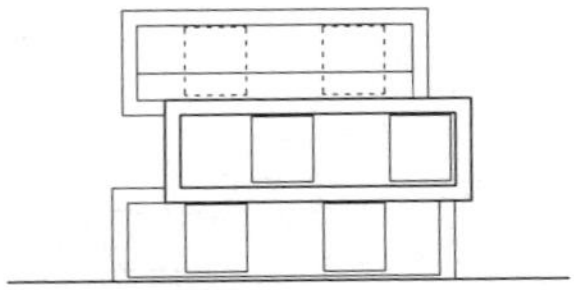

EG

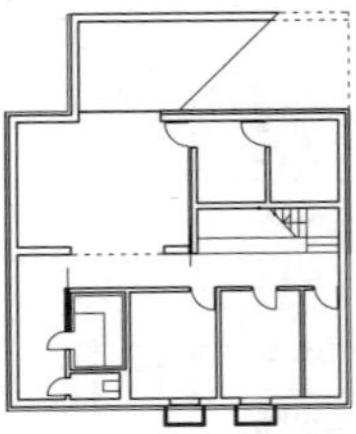

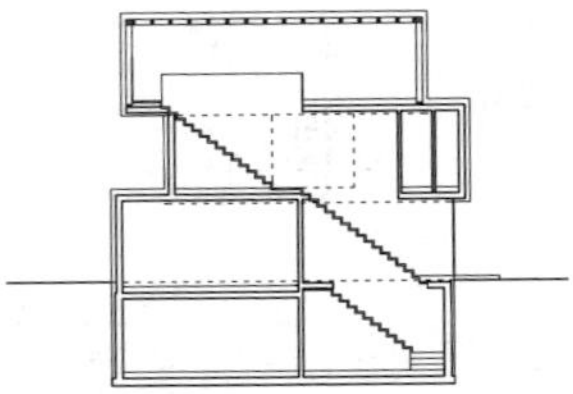

UG

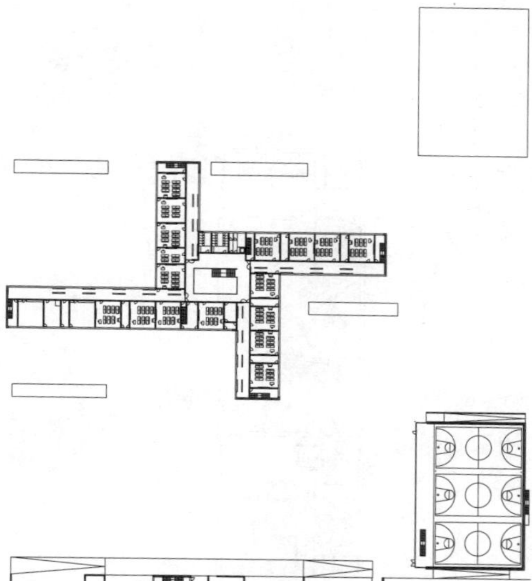

OG

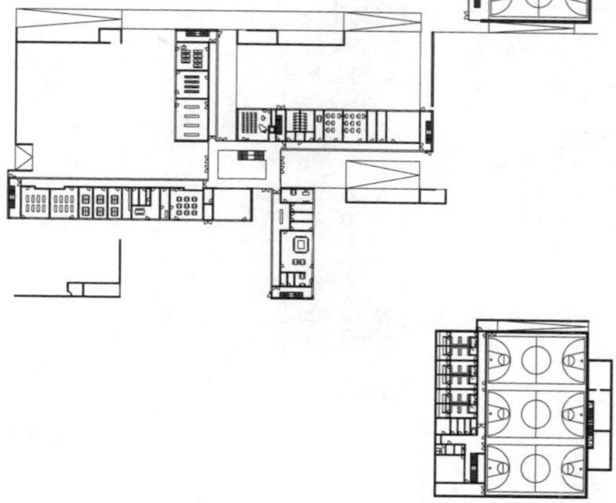

EG

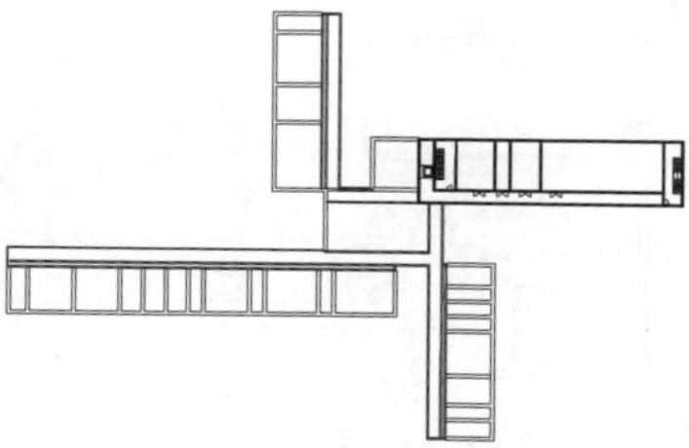

UG

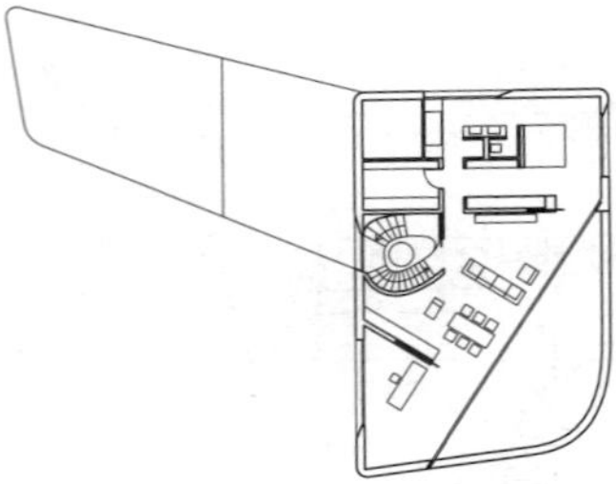

DG

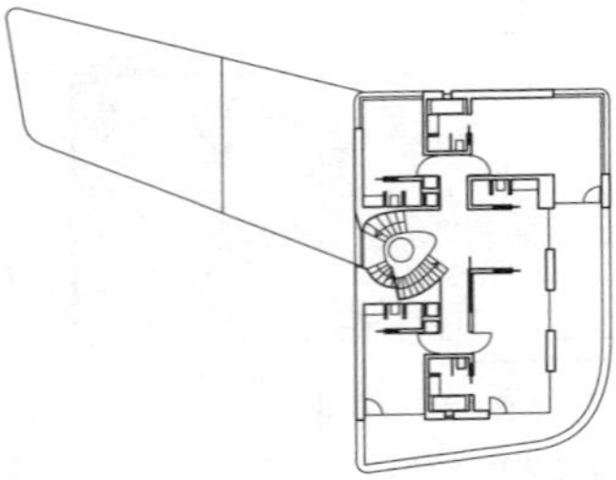

OG

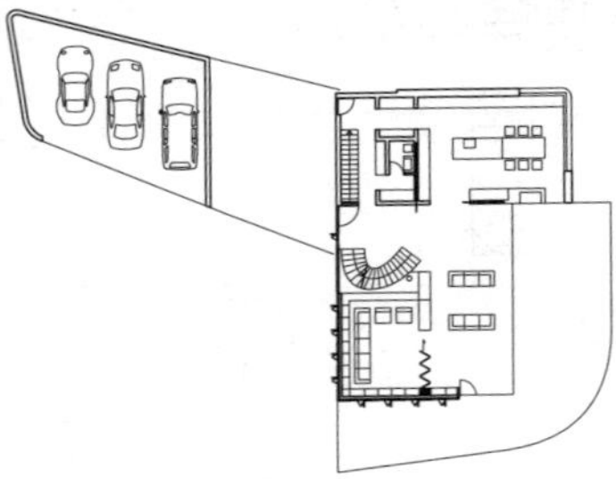

EG

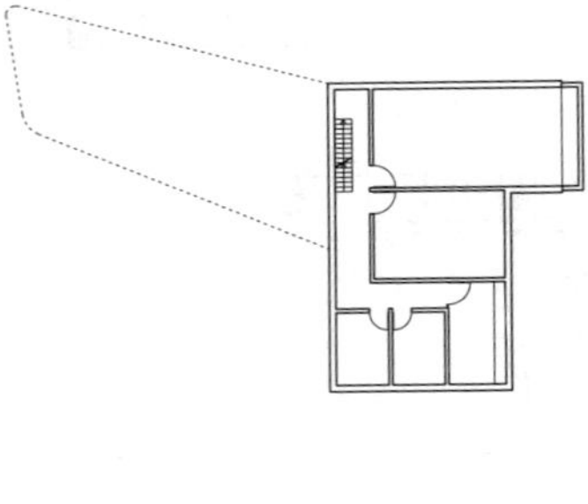

UG

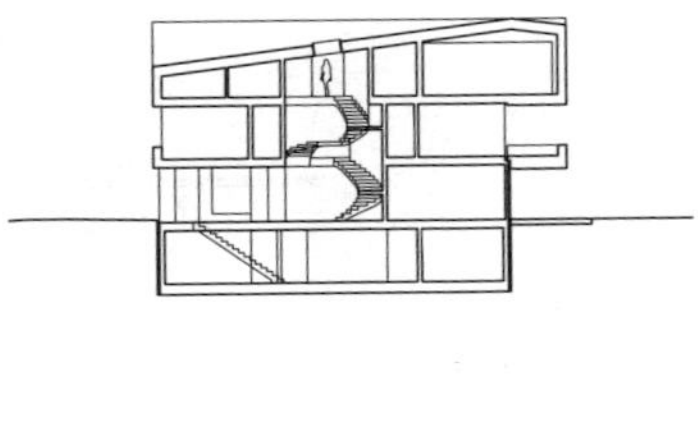

1 : 700

<664

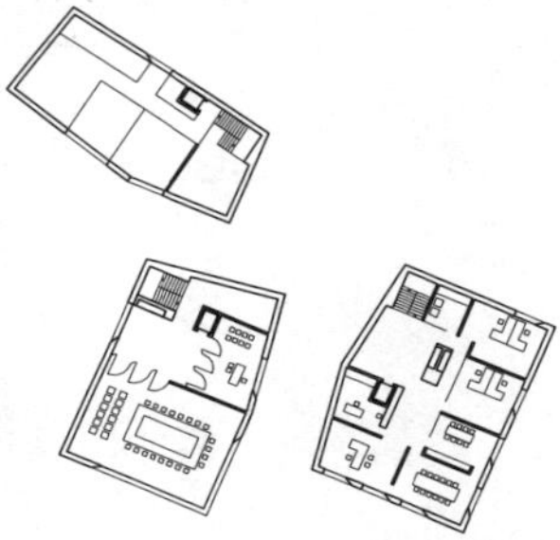

OG

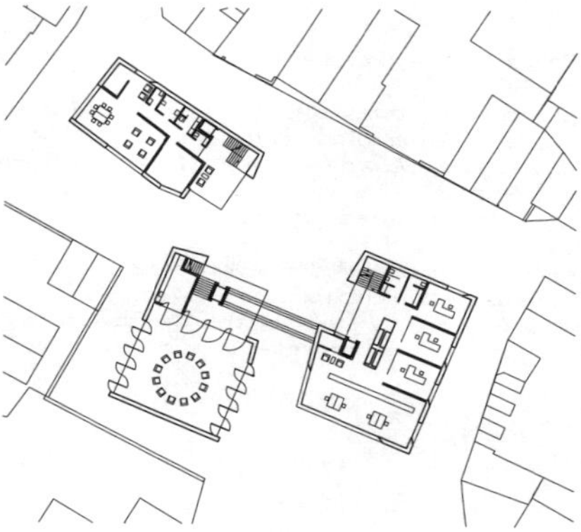

EG

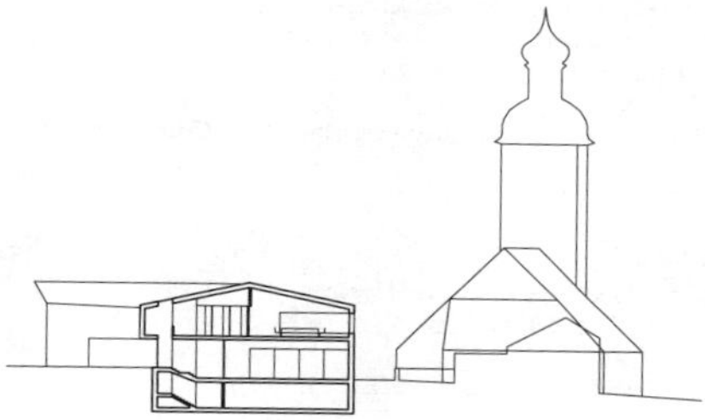

<668

1 : 1250

Felix Bembé, Sebastian Dellinger (Hrsg. | eds)

Bembé Dellinger, Architekten BDA und Stadtplaner, Greifenberg, Deutschland

Printed in Germany
SpringerWienNewYork is a part of
Springer Science + Business Media
springer.at

Graphische Gestaltung | Graphic Design: Denis Klein
Konzept | Concept: Denis Klein, Felix Bembé, Sebastian Dellinger
Übersetzung | Translation: Sharon Heidenreich
Druck | Printed by: Advantage Printpool, Gilching | Germany
Gesetzt in | set in Gill Sans Light | Bold
Satellitenbild | satellite image: Landsat ETM+ Quelle | source: Global Land Cover Facility (GLCF) (mit herzlichem Dank an Hr. Terhalle with thanks to Mr. Terhalle)

Fotografie | Photography
Steffan Müller-Naumann 56-77, 106-113, 128, 218-229, 446-453, 518-533 Johannes Kottje 118-119, 204-206, 208-209 Emanuel Herz 124-127 Dieter Weidlich 129-133 Giovanni Bauer 134-141 Oliver Heissner 144-147, 149-151, 166-167 Thomas Drexel 184-195, 300-305 Boris Storz 264-275 Ricardo Molina 506-511 Ralf Jodl 660-661

Gedruckt auf säurefreiem, chlorfrei gebleichtem Papier – TCF
Printed on acid-free and chlorine-free bleached paper

SPIN: 12783885
Mit zahlreichen Abbildungen | großteils in Farbe
With numerous figures | mostly in colour

Bibliografische Information der Deutschen Nationalbibliothek
Die Deutsche Nationalbibliothek verzeichnet diese Publikation in der Deutschen Nationalbibliografie; detaillierte bibliografische Daten sind im Internet über http://dnb.d-nb.de abrufbar.

ISBN 978-3-7091-0093-6 SpringerWienNewYork